HEALING THE WORLD

WHITEHEAD, FRANCIS, CLARE, AND BONAVENTURE ON SPIRITUAL AND PLANETARY TRANSFORMATION

BRUCE G. EPPERLY

Energion Publications
Gonzalez, Florida
2025

Copyright © 2025, Bruce G. Epperly. All Rights Reserved.

Scripture quotations are taken from the New Revised Standard Version Updated Edition. Copyright © 2021 National Council of Churches of Christ in the United States of America. Used by permission. All rights reserved worldwide.

ISBN: 978-1-63199-946-8
eISBN: 978-1-63199-947-5

Energion Publications
1241 Conference Rd
Cantonment, FL 32533

enerion.com
pubs@enerion.com

TABLE OF CONTENTS

1. Saints in the Making 1
2. Whitehead and Francis 15
3. Whitehead and Clare 37
4. The Fountain of Love 55
5. Healing the Planet 75
6. Instruments of Peace 93
7. Tragic Beauty 111
8. We Are the Ones We've Been Waiting For 133

   Books to Nourish the Spirit 141

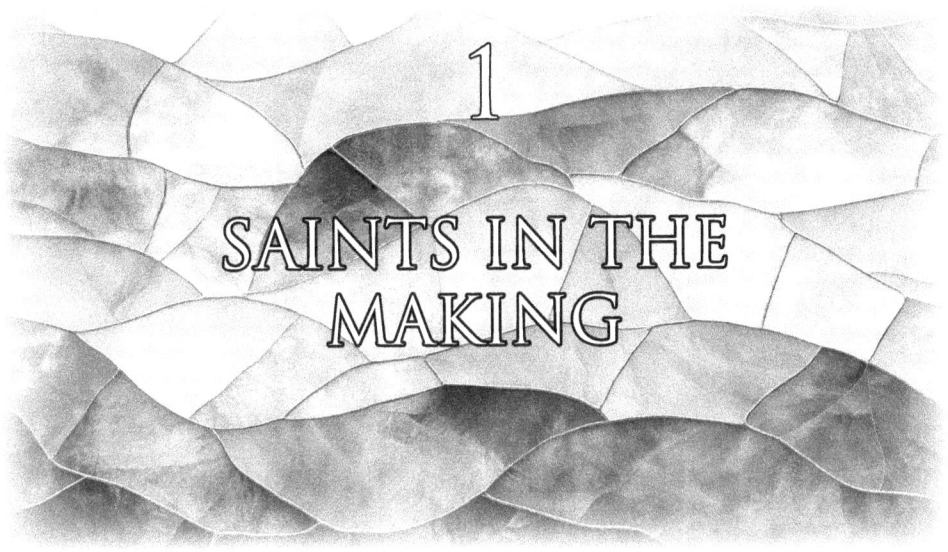

1
SAINTS IN THE MAKING

> *Francis was always new, always fresh, always beginning again. (Thomas of Celeno)*
>
> *The vigour of civilized societies is preserved by the widespread sense that high aims are worthwhile. Vigorous societies harbour a certain extravagance of objectives so that people wander beyond the safe provision of personal gratifications...the perfection of life resides in aims beyond the individual person in question.[1]*

Young Giovanni di Pietro di Bernardone (1181-1226), nicknamed Francesco, or the Frenchman, because of his stylish apparel and lavish lifestyle, was in search of his life's mission. Born to privilege, the son of an upwardly mobile cloth merchant, young Giovanni wanted something more to life than just managing the family business and becoming one of the Italian town of Assisi's elite. He was bright, witty, gregarious, generous, and the life of any party he attended. He serenaded the local maidens and it was assumed that he would eventually find a smart and beautiful wife to ensure further advancement in the upwardly mobile economic and political class to which he belonged. He

---

1 Alfred North Whitehead, *Adventures in Ideas* (New York: Free Press 1933), 288,289.

wanted fame as well as fortune so he went off to war, hoping to achieve knighthood, but was wounded, captured, and then spent months in convalescence pondering his future. During his time of captivity and recovery, the ambitious fun-loving youth was looking not only for physical healing, but the healing of purpose, the spiritual healing that comes from knowing who you are and the nature of your vocation. A healing that comes from knowing the One to whom you owe your ultimate allegiance and then following the path God has set before you.

Francis' prayers for direction in his life were answered. A voice from within as well as from scripture alerted him to a new way of life: a life of simplicity, hospitality, and friendship with all creation. To his father's chagrin, he abandoned the family business, selling all his possessions and leaving Assisi with nothing but the shirt on his back. Though he had reduced his status from riches to rags and privilege to poverty, he found something more valuable than any earthly treasure, alignment with God's vision for his life and unity with God as his ultimate concern.

Down the hill and less than a mile from the village of Assisi lies the Chapel of San Damiano. Still searching and uncertain of the contours of his future, the newly houseless Francis entered the nondescript chapel in search of God's guidance. Gazing at the Cross, Francis heard the voice of Jesus whispering, "Rebuild my church. It has fallen into disrepair." Being a concrete and sensate thinker, Francis initially assumed that God called him to rebuild the dilapidated Chapel of San Damiano and then two other nearby chapels in the vicinity of Assisi. The saint in the making set to the task of refurbishing three chapels brick by brick and beam by beam, spending what little money he had left to bring beauty to God's sanctuaries. Only later did young Francis realize that God called him to a larger mission: to be God's companion in rebuilding and reforming the church of his time and in so doing contribute to the transformation of the world in which he lived. Like the apostle Paul who counseled "do not be conformed to this world, but be transformed by the renewing of the minds so that you may discern the will of God" (Romans 12:2), Francis came to recognize that the inner journey of spiritual transformation was wedded to the outer journey of social and ecclesiastical transformation. In finding God's purpose for his life, he discovered that his vocation was to be an agent of God's vision of a world of justice and peace in which humans lived in harmony with one another and the non-human world. While uninterested in ecclesiastical power and constantly open to creative transformation, Francis' poetry, lifestyle, and values called the Western Church to reformation.

The life and mission of Francis of Assisi has stood the test of time both as an inspiration and challenge. In his ground breaking "Laudato Si," Pope Francis honored Francis of Assisi as the patron saint of ecology. Francis lives on in the quest for spiritual and material simplicity, harmony with nature, embrace of outcasts, and reconciliation with enemies. He deserves St. Bonaventure's affirmation of him as the Second Christ. Not confined to the thirteenth century, Francis models Christ-like living in our time of climate change, international upheaval, and political and social incivility. As his first biographer Thomas of Celano avers, Francis' life became a prayer as his sense of self grew to embrace the whole earth as his home and all creatures as kin.

Encountering Francis and Whitehead. I first encountered Francis as a child when I asked my mother as I gazed on a statue in one of her friend's yards, "Who's that man with the bird on his finger tip?" She responded, "He's a Catholic saint who loved the birds of the air and the lilies of the field." Fifteen years after I met St. Francis as a garden statue, I encountered the philosophy of Alfred North Whitehead (1861-1947). As a religious seeker, recently returned to Christianity and in search of a meaningful vision of God to shape my growing Christian faith, I enrolled in a seminar on process theology, taught by Richard Keady, a student of legendary process theologian John Cobb. In studying Whitehead's philosophical vision, I found a path with a heart and a faith to affirm. I encountered a vision of God that integrated spirituality and social change, honored the environment, and provided hope for persons in crisis, assuring them that God's aim was to heal and not harm. I rediscovered the personal God of my evangelical childhood in the context of a Christ for the Cosmos, who is both Infinite and intimate and Personal and global. A God who can be described as the fellow sufferer who understands and the joyful companion who celebrates.

In deciphering the philosophical language of process theology, I also reclaimed the relational spirit of the hymns of my childhood from a wider perspective, "What a Friend we have in Jesus" and "Jesus loves me, this I know, for the Bible tells me so." In the interplay of Whitehead's philosophy and Francis' reverence for life, I found a faith that soared to the heavens, calling me to go from self-interest to world loyalty, and a concrete earth-oriented spirituality that inspired care for the least of these, whether they are farm workers, houseless persons, Vietnamese refugees and Vietnam era draftees, and endangered species and polluted waterways.

Over the past five decades, my relationship with Whitehead and Francis has grown and has become – like my relationship with Teilhard and Thurman – the lens through which I interpret the world.[2] Whitehead and Francis, along with Teilhard and Thurman, have inspired me to embrace a large spirited Christianity which seeks, as Howard Thurman asserted, to create a friendly world of friendly persons, and challenges me to see Christ's light in all things and be Christ's light in all encounters. The impact of Whitehead and Francis has become ubiquitous in my writing, teaching, relationships, and political involvement. My philosophical, spiritual, and theological journey as a process theologian has been shaped by my encounters with both Thurman and Francis and Francis' spiritual companions Clare and Bonaventure.

Saints in the Making. Did you know that you can aspire, with all humility, to be a saint in the making? Or, if you are of another

---

2   Bruce Epperly, *The God of Tomorrow: Whitehead and Teilhard on Metaphysics, Mysticism, and Mission* (Gonzalez: Energion Publications, 2024.) and *The God of the Growing Edge: Whitehead and Thurman on Theology, Spirituality, and Social Change* (Gonzalez, FL: Energion Publications: 2025).

tradition, a Buddhist Bodhisattva, Hindu mahatma, or Zoroastrian magi in the making. Whitehead and Francis affirm the essential Godward movement of all life. Deep down, all creation sings praises to God, as Francis' "Canticle of the Creatures" (or "Canticle of the Sun") proclaims. Whitehead similarly affirms that the world lives by the incarnation of God. Wherever we are, God is present and we can find, as the panentheistic credo declares:

> God in all things.
> All things in God.

"God in all things" means that recognized or not God is working in your life, calling you to be a companion in healing the world. Even if you are unaware of it, each moment is God breathed and God touched. God's spirit is moving in your cells and in your soul. God is at work aiming at beauty in the human and non-human worlds. The moral and spiritual arcs move through our lives and all creation, urging us to grow in wisdom, stature, and attentiveness to the divine within and the world beyond. There is, as I say in one of my books, "a mystic in you" and a mystic in everyone else. There is a mystic hidden in a prevaricating politician, struggling youth, and overworked parent, waiting to come forth to heal the earth if they but open their hearts and find the right guidance.

Francis of Assisi did not see himself as exceptional. Following the example of Jesus and Jesus' mandate to sell everything and give his possessions to the poor, Francis' path of simplicity was intended to be a model and inspiration for our lives. In our unique ways, depending on our responsibilities and gifts, we too can embrace the good news of "evangelical simplicity," living simply so others may simply live and focusing on God's healing presence in the perpetually perishing world. God calls everyone to sainthood and not the select few that religious traditions describe as saints and mahatmas. We all have the vocation to live by God's incarnation, following the currents of God's inspiration, in our lives.

With God as our companion and guide, we are all saints in the making. Sainthood, or becoming fully human, is not an escape from life's challenges but an embrace of the world in all its tragic beauty. Everyday saintliness involves a willingness to do something beautiful for God by bringing truth, beauty, goodness, love, and justice to the world God loves.

The Roman Catholic activist and mystic, Dorothy Day (1897-1980) protested using the word saint to describe her ministry of spirituality and social action. "Don't call me a saint. I don't want to be dismissed that easily."[3] Day recognized that throughout history saints have been marginalized as so heavenly minded that they viewed as no earthly good! Still, like the saint of Assisi, Dorothy Day believed that God called everyone to spiritual greatness through embodying their faith in daily life. We think small when Jesus calls us to do "greater things." (John 12:12-14) "We are all called to be saints," Day affirmed, "we might as well get over our bourgeois fear of the name. We might also get used to recognizing the fact there is some saint in all of us. Inasmuch as we are growing, putting off the old man and putting on Christ, there is some of the saint, the holy, right here."[4] The omnipresent God is present in the quotidian affairs of our lives and the omniactive God whispers to us at the grocery store, checking our e-mail and social media, and times spent with loved ones.

Saints can be contemplatives. They can also be world changers. They can model what it means to be both heavenly minded and earthly good. They show us what it means to have a vision born of our encounter with God and to incarnate that vision in the world of challenge and conflict, perplexity and promise. Another contemplative activist Simone Weil (1909-1943) boldly challenges persons like us to claim our own saintly and mystical activism:

> Today it is not merely enough to be a saint, but we must have the saintliness demanded by the present moment, a new

---

3 Dorothy Day, *Selected Writings,* edited by Robert Ellsberg (Maryknoll, NY: Orbis Books, 2017), xi.

4 Ibid., xi.

saintliness without precedent…A new type of sanctity is indeed a fresh spring, an invention. If all is kept in proportion and if the order of each thing is preserved, it is almost equivalent to a new revelation of the universe and of human destiny. It is the exposure of a large portion of truth and beauty hitherto concealed under a thick layer of dust.[5]

Right where we are, amid our daily tasks, God calls us to dust off the doors of perception, awaken to the wonder and tragedy of life, and get to work embodying God's call to partnership in healing the earth.

In his time of ecclesiastical opulence, Francis represented a new kind of saint. A follower of Jesus who sought to embody Jesus' mission in the twelfth century world of warring cities, widespread poverty, lackluster worship, crusades and Islamophobia, and papal power and ecclesiastical wealth, Francis presented an alternative vision of spiritual authority, emphasizing the power of love over the love of power and universal hospitality over binary ecclesiology and crusading violence.

As a university student, living almost seven hundred years after Francis' mystical transformation, Whitehead shared his aspiration to "see God" with members of his Cambridge conversation club, the Apostles. In his later years, the philosopher Whitehead described a God-filled universe in which every moment was a portal to experiencing a personal call from an intimate and relational divinity. Whitehead's metaphysics is mystical in spirit and encourages the quest for self-transcendence and world loyalty. For Whitehead, like Francis, peace involves enlarging a person's scope of self-interest to see the well-being of others as essential to one's own well-being. In awakening to God's vision for each moment, described as the "initial aim," we can see God in our lives and be divine messengers to the world around us.

Whitehead and the Parents of Franciscan Spirituality. The spirit of the Franciscan tradition finds its origins in three very different saints, all of whom gave up their economic and political privileges

---
5   Simone Weil, *Waiting for God* (New York: Harper Collins, 2009), 51.

to follow the way of Jesus in their time and place. Francis, the "the little poor one," was an itinerant mystic, whose life shone with the spirit of Jesus in his marriage of mysticism, healing ministry, nature mysticism, and prophetic faith. While Francis did not claim to be a theologian, his life was his message. Francis' commitment to God-intoxicated simplicity, harmony with the non-human world, and hospitality was the inspiration for the movement that bears his name, both as a religious order and a way of life. Francis was the incarnation of Jesus' Sermon on the Mount in his fellowship with outcasts, relationships to the non-human world, and integration of personal and planetary peace. Brother Sun and Sister Moon, not to mention cousin swallow and companion worm, along with the poor of the Earth, were his daily companions. As one of his first biographers, St. Bonaventure, relates, Francis began every sermon with the invocation of God's peace on his congregation and he sought peace with everyone he met, ranging from skeptical church leaders to warring Muslim sultans and boisterous swallows!

Like Francis, St. Clare of Assisi, Clare Offreduccio (1194-1253), gave up prestige and privilege and the promise of wealth and power to embrace Holy Poverty and live out the ministry of the Crucified Jesus. Intelligent and beautiful and the object of devotion of numerous suitors, the "luminous" Clare's spirituality centered on seeing, following, and imitating the life of Jesus. Clare counseled her spiritual followers to "gaze on Jesus," internalize Jesus' spirit, and then "imitate" Jesus' life. Giovanni (John) de Fidanza, St, Bonaventure (1221-1274), the Seraphic Doctor, and contemporary of St. Thomas Aquinas (1225-1274), was the "mind" of the Franciscan movement. A philosopher, theologian and administrator, Bonaventure sought to provide a theological vision grounded in Francis' life. Bonaventure saw God as a fountain of love flowing in and through all things, your life and mine, humankind and the non-human world. A forerunner of panentheism, Bonaventure described God as "an infinite sphere (or circle) whose center is everywhere and whose circumference is nowhere."

God moves in all things, giving life, energy, and purpose to the universe. All things are embraced by God's love and by implication all things are treasured in the heart of God, who feels the joys and sorrows of all creation. Inspired by Francis' vision of unity, Bonaventure sought to mend the schism of Eastern and Western Christianity as well as join monasticism with academic life and institutional maintenance and growth. To paraphrase Whitehead's comments on the expansion of Jesus' mission through the theological commitments of his followers, Francis provided the life of the movement, Clare expanded the circle of holy simplicity to include women as equals created in God's image, and Bonaventure provided a vision, structure, and faithful community grounded in Francis' life of simplicity, unity, interdependence, and holiness.

While Whitehead has yet not been canonized, and may never receive such an ecclesiastical accolade, "Saint Alfred" provides a metaphysical vision that complements, supplements, and integrates Franciscan spirituality with the modern world. Whitehead describes a dynamic, interdependent, value-oriented, and purposive universe, in which God is the reality in whom our lives and all things live, move, and have their being. (Acts 17:28) Whitehead's vision of God provides a contemporary vision of the Franciscan spirit, which inspires our commitments to heal the planet as a whole in terms of ecology, economics, ethnic and personal diversity, and personal and relational spiritual formation.

The New Francis. Today, we need to embody the spirit of a "new Francis," a term attributed to Teilhard de Chardin. We need to be the contemplative activists, saints, mahatmas, magi, and Bodhisattvas of our time. The world is in need of healing and we are called, like Francis, to "repair" the body of Christ, not just the visible church but this Good Earth in all its wondrous, and fragile, variety. This text is an attempt to join the wisdom, mysticism, and practice of Franciscan spirituality with the process theology, spirituality, and social vision emerging from Alfred North Whitehead's philosophical vision to transform the world. We are the ones we have been waiting for, as June Jordan says of the South African women protesting apartheid. We are the ones who are called to incarnate the activist wisdom of St. Francis, Pope Francis, and my own teacher process theologian John Cobb, author of the first book on Christianity and ecology, *Is It Too Late?* With Francis and Whitehead, we are challenged to become agents of new creation and God's partners in healing the Earth. It is my hope and prayer that this text will advance the moral and spiritual arcs of history and inspire us to be earth healers in every aspect of our lives.

I am grateful and give thanks daily for the impact of my "good ancestors" Francis, Clare, Bonaventure, and Whitehead for their inspiration and impact on my writing and life. I am thankful for the leadership of Kelly McCracken, publisher of Franciscan Media, who invited me to write three books on Franciscan spirituality.[6] Henry Neufeld and Chris Eyre at Energion Publications have generously invited me to write this book and have shepherded it to publication. Kate Gould Epperly has been my companion since 1978, and so I say, *ubuntu*, I am because of you, we are because of one another. I dedicate this text to my grandsons Jack and James, to their contemporaries and parents and grandparents from every continent of this and future generations, so that they may raise children who flourish on this Good Earth. I am thankful for the Franciscan and Teilhardian scholarship of Ilia Delio, who in an offhand remark inspired me to write a book on Whitehead and Francis. As I write this book, I feel the pain of children in Gaza, grieving relatives in Israel, anxious parents coming to the United States from Central America, as well as the rise of authoritarian and vitriolic political discourse in the United States, much of it identified falsely with Christianity and guided by manipulative, hard hearted, and prevaricating religious and political leaders. At

---

6   Bruce Epperly, *Walking with Francis of Assisi: From Privilege to Activism* (Cincinnati, OH: Franciscan Media, 2021); *Simplicity, Spirituality, and Service: The Timeless Wisdom of Francis, Clare, and Bonaventure* (Cincinnati; OH: Franciscan Media, 2023); *Head, Heart, and Hands: An Introduction to St. Bonaventure* (Cincinnati, OH: Franciscan Media), 2024.

just such a time like this, we need to embrace the spirit of Francis' message, "May God's peace be with you."

SPIRITUAL PRACTICES FOR GLOBAL HEALERS

Francis and Whitehead saw theology and spirituality as concrete and practical. Our world views and spiritual practices shape our lives and can contribute to the healing of our relationships and the planet. Mysticism leads to mission. Spirituality leads to social transformation. Prayer leads to protest and the visioning of imaginative and concrete alternatives to our personal and corporate alienation from one another and the non-human world. In the spirit of this holistic vision of theology, each chapter concludes with spiritual practices reflecting the spirit of Francis, Clare, Bonaventure, and Whitehead with the goal of embodying their vision in our world view and personal and political lives.

Praying for Peace. As he began each sermon, Francis blessed his congregation, praying that the peace of God be with everyone in attendance. The wandering mystic greeted everyone he met with the salutation, "Peace be with you," and counseled his followers to enter every encounter with the blessing of peace. Accordingly, the quest to join inner and outer peace will be an underlying theme of the spiritual practices found in this text.

As noted earlier, this book emerged in the concreteness of twenty-first century North America. In June 2024, as I write these words of introduction, students protest USA involvement in the war in Gaza, and politicians and peacemakers are confronted with balancing the well-being of Gaza children and the flourishing of Israelis. Politicians spew falsehoods, identify themselves with Jesus' persecution and martyrdom and see themselves as agents of Christian nationalism, promise retribution, and breed incivility and violence. Preachers foment hate against immigrants and the LGBTQ+ community. Despite the USA's current leadership's commitment to responding to climate change, there are signs that what we are doing is "too little, too late." We need, as both Whitehead and Francis assert, to be persons of peace, whose commitment takes us from self-interest to world loyalty and challenges us to see God in all of God's various and often troubling disguises.

Although it is unlikely that St. Francis penned the prayer popularly known as "The Prayer of St. Francis," this prayer reflects the spirit of the twelfth century saint as well as Whitehead's counsel to become large souled persons, who see the well-being of others and our well-being as intricately connected. This prayer can become a guidepost for daily life and social involvement and an inspiration to creating an alternative vision of politics and decision-making.

> Lord, make me an instrument of Your peace;
> Where there is hatred, let me sow love;
> Where there is injury, pardon;
> Where there is doubt, faith;
> Where there is despair, hope;
> Where there is darkness, light;
> And where there is sadness, joy.
> O Divine Master,
> Grant that I may not so much seek
> To be consoled as to console;
> To be understood, as to understand;
> To be loved, as to love;
> For it is in giving that we receive,
> It is in pardoning that we are pardoned,
> And it is in dying that we are born to Eternal Life.

Take time to read and pray these words daily. You may abbreviate them simply to "God, make me an instrument of peace," as I do as I begin my daily predawn walk. Breathe deeply as read these words, experiencing your connectedness with every life form and overcoming your sense of alienation from your fellow humans and the non-human world. Silently invoke, "peace be with you," as you greet family members, friends, checkout clerks, and in every encounter, both intentional and random. Commit yourself to becoming a peace seeker in the challenges and contrasts of life.

Seeing God. As a young person, Whitehead had an aspiration toward encountering the Holy, "I want to see God." The quest for experiencing the Holy motivated much of Whitehead's later philosophical quest. Both Francis and Whitehead describe a God-filled world. Yet God is often hidden from our experience, perhaps due to God's ubiquity, that is, in the same way that we don't notice the air we breathe or the spiritual waters in which we swim, or perhaps due to our lack of focus on the beauty of the Earth or our emphasis on our personal desires to the detriment of our relationships to the world around us and the divinity hidden in all things.

Similar to the first exercise, I invite you to begin with Whitehead's prayer, "I want to see God." Then listen for God's still, small voice whispering in your inner experience and the events of your life. Further, in the spirit of the Prayer of St. Francis, look throughout the day for the divinity and holiness in those around you. A North African mystic asserted that the monk is all eye. In that spirit, be all sense: awakening yourself throughout the day to the holiness of the moment, the sacrament of this one unrepeatable moment of your "wild and precious life," as poet Mary Oliver counsels. Breathe deeply. Look deeply. Awaken to the holiness of yourself and others and, as social activist Dorothy Day noted, speak to persons as if they are angels, revealers of God in all their wondrous and unique imperfection. Speak to your political leaders by phone calls or emails advocating for peace and justice, with the affirmation of their holiness and God's movements in their lives. Let your words and actions witness to the moral and spiritual arcs of divine presence flowing through your life to others and through all things to you.

WHITEHEAD AND FRANCIS

A WORLD OF PRAISE

The teleology of the universe is aimed at the production of beauty.[1]

*Be praised, my Lord, through all your creatures,
especially through my lord Brother Sun,
who brings the day; and you give light through him.
And he is beautiful and radiant in all his splendor!
Of you, Most High, he bears the likeness…*

*Praised be You, my Lord, through Sister Mother Earth,
who sustains us and governs us and who produces
varied fruits with colored flowers and herbs….*[2]

Whitehead and the founders of the Franciscan movement – Francis, Clare, and Bonaventure – call us to vocational and spiritual transformation on a personal, political, and global scale. We need big ideas, wise strategies, and

---

1   Alfred North Whitehead, *Adventures of Ideas* (New York: Free Press, 1933), 265.
2   Found in Murray Bodo, *The Journey and the Dream* (Cincinnati: Franciscan Media, 2011), 169-170.

great compassion to heal the world. We also heal the world one moment and encounter at a time. One moment can, as Francis experienced, change everything. We can repair the church, which has fallen away from the teachings of Jesus and become an instrument of alienation and violence, and then begin repairing the world. A small group of people dedicated to healing the world can turn the tide from destruction and violence to repair and reconciliation. Whitehead and the Franciscan founders call us to become saints for our time. Although I speak of the need for the "new Francis," individually and collectively, I am reminded of the Jewish proverb: "When the Messiah comes, the Messiah won't ask if you were David, but were you fully yourself as God's companion in bringing forth the Messianic age of Shalom, healing, and peace?" How can I, Bruce Epperly, claim my vocation as a humble world healer? How can you, my reading companion, join me in healing the Earth and its creatures? How can religious institutions of every faith tradition become instruments of peace, putting love ahead of power and hospitality ahead of dogma? Finite and imperfect as we are, we are God's beloved, and we matter in moving the moral and spiritual arcs of the universe forward. For Francis and Whitehead, spiritual transformation involves the insight that we are living in an enchanted, value-laden, interdependent, and God-filled universe. We are living in a world of praise. Spiritual transformation involves finite persons like us devoting our head, hearts, and hands to God's vision of Shalom one moment and act at a time.

FRANCIS' WORLD OF PRAISE

For Francis, the monk, the monastic is not just all eye – and deep down, all of us are monastics in the making, called to be God's agents of healing and peace – but all sense, including intuition and paranormal experiences. The world is filled with God's glory (Isaiah 6:1-8), as Isaiah discovers, and the beauties of the Earth reflect and remind us of Divine Beauty. The self-transcen-

Healing the World

dence of mysticism draws us toward rather than away from the world and inspires us to treat worldly things with heavenly love. Francis' vision is revealed in his Canticle of the Creatures, expanding on the sentences that introduced this chapter.

> Be praised, my Lord, through all your creatures,
> especially through my lord Brother Sun,
> who brings the day; and you give light through him.
> And he is beautiful and radiant in all his splendor!
> Of you, Most High, he bears the likeness.
> Praise be You, my Lord, through Sister Moon
> and the stars, in heaven you formed them
> clear and precious and beautiful.
> Praised be You, my Lord, through Brother Wind,
> and through the air, cloudy and serene,
> and every kind of weather through which
> You give sustenance to Your creatures.
> Praised be You, my Lord, through Sister Water,
> which is very useful and humble and precious and chaste.
> Praised be You, my Lord, through Brother Fire,
> through whom you light the night and he is beautiful
> and playful and robust and strong.
> Praised be You, my Lord, through Sister Mother Earth,
> who sustains us and governs us and who produces
> varied fruits with colored flowers and herbs....
> Praised be You, my Lord,
> through our Sister Bodily Death,
> from whom no living man can escape....
> Praise and bless my Lord,
> and give Him thanks
> and serve Him with great humility.[3]

Praise is a matter of voice and vision. Of experiencing holiness and sharing holiness and wholeness with the world. As I write these words in mid-June 2024, I am sitting in a Costa Brava,

---

3 Ibid., 169-170.

Spain, coffee house, taking a break from my participation in a cultural tour and basketball tournament in which my thirteen-year-old son is participating with other boys from the Maryland suburbs and teams from throughout Europe and the British Isles. While I reflect and put words to page, I experience the background music and the babble of the community of patrons. I delight in the aroma of espresso being brewed, the sound of various languages, some of which are unfamiliar to me, and the unique and diverse humanity that passes by my wing chair and coffee table. I feel the sea air as I experience the calm rhythm of the waves. I embrace and give thanks for the world of praise in this Catalonian coffee house. Each person is unique, valued, and beloved by their Creator. We know we are broken, and so is our earth, but we are also, as my wife's spiritual director affirms, beloved and blessed, each person deep down revealing the movements of the Wise Creativity that gives birth to galaxies, planets, the slow process of evolution, and each new day. With the Greek philosopher Pythagoras, if we train our senses and our spirit, we can hear the music of the spheres vibrating beneath the voices and the popular music. We can feel the spirit of Francis' Canticle moving in our spirits and joining all creation with its Creator, and each creature with its environment.

Francis experiences an enchanted world in which all things have the potential to praise God. When Francis proclaimed, "God and all things," he asserted that the whole world was in the care of a loving God and that the living God gives life to all things from worms and fiery sparks to popes and parents. The universe is alive, part and whole. Trees clap their hands and invite insects to promote their growth and in turn provide sustenance for their insect companions. Flowers lure bees and bees return home to their hives to make honey, pollinating along the way. The birds of the air sing praises, and the lilies of the field burst forth out of joy and claim their vocation as beauty makers. Right Whales and Humpbacked Whales sing and dance. Babies learn to walk and grow up to be world changers. We are part of this wondrous, diverse, value-filled, and God loved planet and the universe around us.

Francis proclaimed a world of value and experience. In the stories of Francis' ministry to the non-human world, we discover that birds preach sermons and take seriously the preacher's need for silence. A vicious wolf listens to reason and ceases to terrorize the community of Gubbio. Just as miraculous, the people of Gubbio abandon their feelings of fear and anger, renounce violence, and welcome the wolf into the community as its companion and protector. Francis believed that we have the obligation to share good news with the non-human world. According to his first biographer, Thomas of Celeno, once, after preaching a sermon to the birds, Francis "accused himself of negligence because he had not preached to them before." In years to come, Francis "carefully exhorted all birds, all animals, all reptiles, and also insensible creatures, to praise and love the Creator, because daily, invoking the name of the Savior, he observed their obedience in his own experience."[4]

Francis saw a reciprocity between humans and the non-human world in which we are teachers of one another. Jesus asked us to learn from the birds of the air and the lilies of the field, and Francis found guidance in the simple trust and faithful praise of our companion animals. He also believed in a congruence between humans and non-humans in which humans could be teachers of their non-human companions. While preparing to give a sermon, Francis noticed that swallows were chirping with such great joy that his human audience could not hear his words. Francis counseled his swallow kin, "My sister swallows, now it is the time for me to speak, since you have already said enough. Listen to the word of the Lord and stay quiet and calm until the word of the Lord is completed." And verily the sparrows listened with reverence and attention rivaling that of his human audience.[5]

---

4 Francis of Assisi, *Francis of Assisi: The Saint – The Early Documents* (New York: New City Press, 1999), 235.
5 Ibid., 235.

Scripture challenges to honor all creation. After reading the words, "I am a worm and not a man," Francis began to see worms as holy and treat them with reverence similar in spirit to the Jain religious tradition. Thomas of Celano notes: "that is why he used to pick them up from the road and put them in a safe place so that they would not be crushed by the footsteps of passersby."[6] Thomas of Celano adds:

> Fields and vineyards,
> Rocks and woods,
> all the beauties of the field,
> flowing springs and gardens,
> earth and fire, air and wind;
> all these he urged to love of God and to willing service.
> Finally, he used to call all creatures
> by the name of "brother" and "sister"
> and in a wonderful way, unknown to others,
> he could discern the secrets of the heart of creatures
> like someone who had already passed
> into the freedom of the glory of the children of God.[7]

We live in a world of praise in which all creatures, and rocks and trees, are kin. Francis was a mystic, shaman, and animal whisperer long before the words "panpsychism" and "panexperientialism" came into vogue in theological circles. His world was alive and enchanted. Like the Celtic spiritual guides, he perceived thin places everywhere and in all things. Francis even had a special affinity to the coals and sparks of fires, believing that the light of God shone through them as well. Centuries before Teilhard de Chardin, Francis lived with the awareness of the "within," the inner energy of love, embedded in all things, from rocks to sovereigns.

Centuries later, Albert Schweitzer used the phrase "reverence for life" to describe what Francis found in his honoring of the

---

6   Ibid., 250.
7   Ibid., 251.

non-human world. Our relationship to the non-human world should reflect the power of love and the joy of kinship and not the power of manipulation and alienation. Our vocation as companions of God and the non-human world is to repair and not destroy, whether this involves our neighbor, political "opponents," or the Good Earth that is our Mother and Kin.

In everyday life, we as a culture objectify nature and demonize our fellow humans. We prize profit over planetary and personal wellbeing, and power over justice. Difference often leads to division and the destruction of otherness, whether that otherness involves level of intelligence, physical and mental acuity, and health condition as well as race, gender, sexual identity, ethnicity, citizenship, and nation of origin. Francis' mystical experiences led him to believe that there is no "other." Divinity is the deepest reality of all creation. There is, as the Quakers affirm, something of God in everyone. God loves the least of these as well as the greatest, and as you have done unto the least of these, you have done unto God (Matthew 25:32-45).

Throughout his life, Francis was committed to widening his circle of love. Although he was generous with alms in relationship to persons with serious skin diseases, Francis was deathly afraid of persons with leprosy. Proximity elicited anxiety until Francis realized that lepers were God's beloved children. He discovered that persons with leprosy were, as Mother (Saint) Teresa says, God in God's distressing disguises. They are God's call to community and humanity. Filled with God's love for persons with leprosy, Francis embraced and kissed a "leper," and despite his initial fear, Francis became known as the patron saint of persons with leprosy.

Francis believed that differences in politics and religion are calls to conversation and reconciliation not denunciation and destruction. In 1219, Francis was present at one of the pope's military crusades in Northern Egypt. During a time of truce between the Christians and Muslims, Francis crossed boundaries of religious loyalty and nationalism to share the way of Jesus with Sultan Malik al-Kamil. Although Francis failed in his quest to convert the Sultan, he and the Sultan became friends, listening to one another's witnesses and respecting each other's spirituality. In a time of mutual suspicion, hatred, and violence, not unlike our own time of incivility and political violence, xenophobia, and alienation, Francis and the Sultan broke down religious barriers and experienced the holiness of one another as they engaged in interfaith dialogue.

Francis was a mystic and not an academic philosopher or theologian. However, Francis' life and writings reveal a living, enchanted universe, in which life in its wondrous diversity is interdependent and creative and God is the ultimate source of cosmic enchantment. We can praise God because God is moving in our lives and all creation. Creation is, as later theologians asserted, the primary word of God, prior to scripture, because God breathes in and through all things. Our task is not to dominate or destroy but to value the many faces of divine artistry. Everything has value as a center of experience revealing the handiwork of the Poet of the Universe, described seven centuries later by Whitehead. We are always on holy ground and what is holy deserves our reverence and respect.

Francis aspired to see the world as Jesus did, full of life, love, and wonder, and worthy of our affirmation and healing touch. With cleansed doors of perception, Francis, following his Savior, saw each creature as a word and wonder of divine love. According to his biographer Thomas of Celano, Francis was:

> Always with Jesus,
> Jesus in his heart,
> Jesus in his mouth,
> Jesus in his ears,
> Jesus in his eyes,
> Jesus in his hands,
> Jesus in his whole body.[8]

---

8   Francis of Assisi, *Francis of Assisi: The Saint – Early Documents*, 283.

In Francis' world of praise, our cells and souls join with all creation in praising the Creator, whose love and wisdom give birth to all things.

WHITEHEAD'S RELATIONAL UNIVERSE

Is nature lifeless or alive? That is the question Whitehead posed in his final full-length book *Modes of Thought*. How we answer this question may shape our religion, politics, economics, and the future of our planet.

A lifeless universe is the material for human fabrication and domination. If we believe nature cannot feel or experience the Holy, then nothing is off limits in our use of the natural world and its creatures. Unrestrained production, whether prompted by capitalism, state socialism, or communism, leads to climate change, environmental devastation, and species extinction along with the widening gap between wealthy and impoverished. A lifeless universe is also a godless universe. If God is present at all in a lifeless and mechanistic world, then God must act supernaturally from the outside, miraculously violating the predictable laws of nature. Ironically, authoritarian religious leaders often privilege a lifeless universe in which God speaks only through limited ecclesiastical and sacramental channels that they deem to be God's only conduits to our fallen world over a living God filled universe in which all creation can praise God. If the world is clearly divided between spheres of revelation and spheres of darkness, autocrats, authoritarians, and fundamentalists can claim to be the only vehicles of truth and patriotism, and define their opponents as traitors and heretics, undeserving of any ethical consideration. In contrast, if the universe is alive, and characterized by a variety of levels of experience, then all creatures, each in their own way, experience the Holy, can tell about it, and deserve a voice in shaping the world. In a world of praise, experience, and value, the church and its priesthood are but one vehicle of revelation in a living, God-filled world. Despite differing levels of experience and fidelity, all creatures are touched by God and deserve respect and ethical treatment. The denunciation and in many cases destruction of pagan, earth based, and indigenous religious sites and ostracism of Earth oriented and matriarchal spiritualities is often the direct result of authoritarian visions of God and narrow understandings of revelation, experience, value, and life. As Jesus asserted, God's sun and rain fall on the righteous and unrighteous, and also the human and non-human (Matthew 5:25; 6:25-34).

While we cannot go back to the pre-scientific age, we can move forward toward a reenchanted scientific, spiritual, and theological partnership, grounded in the view that spirits are embodied and bodies are inspired, whether are speaking of the relationships of cells to one another, distant or nonlocal causation often described by the faithful as prayer, the influence of thoughts on personal wellbeing, and the growing use of energetic forms of healing. Moreover, as I noted earlier, there is growing evidence that trees interact with their environment, insects and plants cooperate with one another, crows can solve puzzles that would baffle a five-year-old human, and the growth of plants may be influenced by a positive spiritual environment. "In rustling grass, I hear God pass. God speaks to me everywhere."[9]

Experience is Everywhere and Relationship is Everything. Whitehead visualizes a living, value-laden, purposive, energetic, dynamic, and interdependent universe grounded in the movements of a lively, appreciative, purposive, energetic, dynamic, and relational God. At the heart of Whitehead's metaphysical vision are a number of interconnected factors characterizing reality, part and whole: interdependence, experience, value, creativity, order and novelty, and divinity. God is both the primary exemplar and parent of these characteristics insofar as God is present as the ground of purpose, value, and energy in the universe. Neither beginning nor ending, the relationship of God and the world is always characterized by creativity, interdependence, and transformation, in which the Creator's vision, ex-

---

9   Maltbie Babcock, "This is My Father's World." (1901)

perience, and agency emerges in relationship to the lively and dynamic universe. There is never a break between God and the world. As the mantra of panentheism, similar to Francis "God and all things," proclaims:

> God in all things.
> All things in God.

God is the heart of creation and the spirit moving in all things. Creation is the companion of God, enriching God's experience and providing God with new opportunities for creativity in response to the tragic beauty of personal, national, and global history. God and creation, in the movements of cosmic creativity, share a dance of intimacy, agency, teleology, and sensitivity.

Whitehead notes that the whole universe conspires to create each moment of experience. Experience and relatedness go hand in hand. We are connected and in our connection with God and one another, our experience of the world and ourselves emerges. Every moment emerges from its immediate and far off predecessors and contributes to the quality of experience of its immediate successors and the long-term historical arc. Whitehead notes that in many ways "everything is everywhere at all times."[10] Like Francis, Whitehead saw no gap between God and the world and the human and non-human worlds. In the spirit of the Southern African affirmation, ubuntu, we can affirm "I am because of you. We are because of one another." In an interdependent universe, there is no "other" foreign to me. The birds of the air and the lilies of the field shape my experience. As I walk the neighborhood streets of suburban Washington DC in the predawn hours, bird songs inspire contemplation and creativity, and my footsteps shape the accents of their melodies. I am connected with the immigrant family heading north to seek asylum in the United States and the MAGA hatted crusader fearful that undocumented residents will

---

10 Alfred North Whitehead, *Science and the Modern World* (New York: Free Press, 1967), 91.

threaten white privilege. I am one with an emerging galaxy and a recently conceived fetus. Deep down, nothing and no person is foreign to me. Nor is anything foreign to God. God does not leap supernaturally across a chasm to come to a lifeless and insentient Earth. God is incarnate everywhere and in everything from cells to souls, and dogs to dolphins. "Creation sings and around me rings the music of the spheres."

We live in an experiential universe. Each moment of experience feels its universe, shaping itself in accordance with its positive or negative response to the environment. While there are gradations of experience from the simplest quanta to human and angelic experience, the world is alive. A living universe invites us to experience the holiness of sparks from a fire, swallows singing, wolves howling, and babies crying. In a world of experience, all things are touched by God and bear God's incarnation. All creatures can also raise their voices, each in their own unique way, to praise God. Whitehead, like Francis and his spiritual companions, would feel at home with the words of Psalm 148 and 150.

> Praise the LORD!
> Praise the LORD from the heavens;
>   praise God in the heights!
> Praise God, all God's angels;
>   praise God, all God's host!
> Praise him, sun and moon;
>   praise him, all you shining stars!
> Praise him, you highest heavens,
>   and you waters above the heavens!
> Let them praise the name of the LORD,
>   for God commanded and they were created.
> God established them forever and ever;
>   God fixed their bounds, which cannot be passed.
> Praise the LORD from the earth,
>   you sea monsters and all deeps,

> fire and hail, snow and frost,
>> stormy wind fulfilling his command!
> Mountains and all hills,
>> fruit trees and all cedars!
> Wild animals and all cattle,
>> creeping things and flying birds!
> Kings [queens and leaders] of the earth and all peoples,
>> princes [and princesses] and all rulers of the earth!
> Young men and women alike,
>> old and young together!
> Let them praise the name of the LORD,
>>> for God's name alone is exalted;
>>> God's glory is above earth and heaven…
> Let everything that breathes praise God.

"Let everything that breathes praise God." Swallows and wolves praise God, infants and elders praise God, and, as process theologian Jay McDaniel notes, even the stars pray. All creation lives in relationship with God, and to be in relationship requires mutuality of experience. God feels the universe, moment by moment and creature by creature, and the universe, micro and macro, feels God giving it life, purpose, and energy.

A Value Laden Universe. To exist is to experience, and to experience is to be of value. Every creature, from the wolf of Gubbio to the worm that Francis protected as he walked the paths of Umbria, is of value to itself, to God, and to the universe. In many ways, the universe is the "body of God," reflecting divine wisdom and energy. Whitehead asserts that the world lives by the incarnation of God. God's presence gives – and affirms – value in all things. God is present in each creature and each and every creature deserves reverence as God's creation and expression. Even when we go astray, devaluing ourselves and others, we are still of value to ourselves, the planet, and to the all-embracing and all-loving Creative Wisdom of the Universe. God loves the lost sheep as well as the ninety-nine safe in the fold. Indeed, the healing of the universe requires embracing and welcoming the hundredth and every other lost sheep as valuable and necessary to the well-being of the Whole, so that God will be "all in all." (I Corinthians 15:28) God feels the joy and pain of the world, human and non-human alike.

Tradition and Innovation. The process is the reality and the reality is adventurous. Whitehead asserts that the aim of the universe is toward the production of beauty. The achievement of God's aim involves the constant interplay of past, present, and future; order and novelty; and tradition and innovation. God is the principle of order and also the restless spirit of change. Novelty means nothing – and can produce nothing meaningful – apart from a framework of order and past history. Similarly, order without innovation stagnates and atrophies. The prophetic call to creative transformation may appear chaotic and threatening to the champions of the status quo and backward-looking politics and religion. Indeed, the pure conservative, struggling to maintain yesterday's religion and culture, Whitehead asserts, is going against the nature of the universe and God's vision of Shalom. God is the ultimate source of cosmic and planetary evolution and the prophetic moral and spiritual arc of history. While honoring our greatest achievements in science, medicine, history, religion, and human rights, God also says *plus ultra,* "there is more" to be achieved in furthering God's moral and spiritual arcs. God's faithfulness is found in the stability of the seasons and also in the divine mercies and creative spirit that is "new every morning." (Lamentations 3:22-23)

Universal Agency. While Francis did not articulate a theology of human and non-human agency, both Francis and Whitehead affirm that we can turn toward or away from God's vision of our lives. We can be agents of repairing the church and healing the world and also destroyers of land, earth, and sea.

Whitehead sees creativity and self-determination as universal. God's love is uncontrolling, as theologian Thomas Jay Oord avers.[11] It does not envy, but supports, affirms, and promotes creative freedom. In fact, agency is built into the nature of reality. Within the limits imposed by the past, God is free and so are we. We are all agents of adventurous creativity and artists of experience, using the materials life gives us and the results of previous decisions, to shape our lives and the world beyond us. God may be, as Isaiah 64:8 asserts, the potter who shapes the contours of our lives, and yet God, like the potter, must work with the uniqueness of the clay, adapting to us just as we respond to God. Freedom and creativity are real and built into the nature of the universe, enabling us to be agents of creation or destruction. While God often deals with the ambiguity and harm created by our decisions, God constantly says to us, "Create in freedom and love. Surprise me with new creation." As Mother (Saint) Teresa says, our real agency, our ability to bring something new into the world, enables us to do something beautiful for God.

The Empathetic, Sensate, and Relational God. God is the primary exemplification and source of the interdependence, dynamism, creativity, agency, order, novelty, and value of the universe. My teachers John Cobb and David Griffin describe God in terms of creative-responsive love. God is present in every moment of experience as the inspiration to creative transformation. God provides the initial vision and energy for every process of self-creation. As such, God is constantly creating the universe due to God's ever-incarnation in each moment of experience. Without beginning or end, God is fabricating the universe part and whole. God's creativity is aimed at nurturing the highest possibilities of creaturely creativity. The exemplar and engine of uncontrolling love at every level of existence, God invites us to be as creatively loving as possible in terms of our own personal agency. God shapes all things without controlling all things. Freedom is real and built into the divinely inspired universe "from the very beginning."

---

11   Thomas Jay Oord, *The Uncontrolling Love of God: An Open and Relational Account of Providence* (Nampa, Idaho: SacraSage Press, 2015).

A God who is constantly doing a new thing and constantly growing in relationship to the world is more alive and ultimately more influential in the world than a God who determines and predestines all things. In contrast, an omnipotent, predetermining God cannot change or initiate new possibilities and is locked eternally into God's initial timeless vision of the universe. A living God is the "most moved mover," as Abraham Joshua Heschel states, energizing and inspiring all things and being influenced by all things. God gives birth to each moment of experience and each moment of experience has an impact on God. A relational God inspires and promotes creaturely creativity. In stark contrast to the lively relational God, the unilateral and omnipotent God acts but doesn't listen, demands but does not honor, and determines but does not empathize. The relational God's "eye is on the sparrow," as the spiritual says, and "I know God watches me." God feels our joy and pain, responds to our deepest concerns, and hears our prayers. Although God's love is uncontrolling, God's empathetic love is constantly at work in our lives seeking the highest possibility for wholeness and creativity, given our environment and previous decisions. God never gives up on any creature in God's quest for the "best for that impasse," every moment of our lives as individuals and as planetary citizens.

As most moved mover, God is the ultimate recipient of value. God's love and empathy are universal and without limit. In God's "consequent nature," God receives the totality of the universe in each immediate moment, treasuring it everlastingly, and using what can be salvaged to achieve God's vision of Shalom, peace and harmony of all creation. God is, Whitehead affirms, the fellow sufferer who understands and the joyous companion who celebrates. As a hymn of my Baptist childhood affirms,

> What a friend we have in Jesus,
> All our sins and griefs to bear.

> What a privilege to carry
> Everything to God in prayer.[12]

God is here and God is near. Everything has a home in God and all creatures are inspired by God. As mystics throughout the ages, including Francis, Clare, and Bonaventure, note, God is nearer to me than my next breath and in aligning with God's presence, feeling our oneness with God and creation, our own scope of freedom and creativity expands. Like Jesus, God wants us to "grow in wisdom and stature." (Luke 2:52) God wants us to be "fully human," lovingly creative, so that we might become as fully divine as possible bearing God's creative-responsive love in our own lives and ethical commitments.

SPIRITUAL PRACTICES FOR GLOBAL HEALERS

Francis and Whitehead invite us to live in a God filled universe. We can experience God's presence through gazing at photographs from the Hubble and Webb telescopes. We can also discover God's incarnation in a grandchild, lifelong companion, political opponent, firefly, or pangolin. God is, as the apostle Paul proclaims in his universalist sermon preached at the Areopagus in Athens, the reality "in whom we live and move and have our being." (Acts 17:28) God makes Godself known to every people and creature. Yet, the ever-present is often the ever- hidden. There is always more to God than we can imagine. God's transcendence is found in God's universality, ubiquity, empathy, infinity, and eternality. We need, as William Blake counsels, to cleanse the doors of perception so that we can experience the Infinite in the finite and move from isolation and division to praise and affirmation. The following global healing practices focus on cleansing our perception through seeing and praising the Creative and Loving Wisdom in whom we live and move and have our being.

---

12 Joseph Scriven, "What a Friend We Have in Jesus." (1855).

Seeing God in All Things. Francis often proclaimed, "God and all things." The mystic from Assisi was a forerunner of the panentheist affirmation "God in all things." These affirmations ground us in the concrete "sacrament of the present moment," described by Jesuit spiritual guide Pierre de Caussade. (1675-1751) Each moment is a sacramental portal into the Holy. For those with eyes to see, there are "thin places" everywhere and in everyone. In this spiritual practice, simply live by Whitehead's youthful and later philosophical affirmation, "I want to see God," or Francis' quest to experience "Jesus in his ears, Jesus in his eyes, Jesus in his hands, Jesus in his whole body."

Once again, let us go deeper with the simple prayer, made throughout the day, "I want to see God" or "I want to see with Jesus' eyes." You may want to concretize this to "I want to see God in this person" or "I want to see God in this situation." On a morning in June 2024, as I walked the streets of Barcelona, Spain, on a cultural and youth basketball holiday with my son, grandson, and parents and children from suburban Maryland, my prayer was "I want to see God in every face." On my solitary walk down the Gran Via Les Corts Catalanes, I peered into each passing early morning face. Though only a few walkers acknowledged my presence, I sought to see the divine in them. Though far from my Washington DC suburban home, I found myself feeling at home on this unfamiliar boulevard. Wherever I am, God is present. Inspired by experiencing God's presence on a Barcelona boulevard, I took to my computer and penned several paragraphs that you are reading today.

Returning home from holiday, I sought to see God's presence in the scrum and chaos of USA politics, especially in politicians in whom God's presence appears most absent to me. The prayer "I want to see God" joins the interior and exterior, the contemplative and sensate, the friend and foe, as one reality. The journey inward is the journey outward. Our moment-by-moment self-creation is also our gift to the world.

In this exercise, listen first to the Godward spirit in yourself: see and affirm the Holy as your deepest reality. "You are the light of the world. God's image shines in you. You are beloved in all your brokenness." You don't need to be ashamed, afraid, or anxious, nor do you need to feel shame or inferiority. God is in you, providing loving possibilities, just as you are. Deep down, God is with you and God is in you. In the spirit of God's words to Jesus as he rose after his baptism, "You are God's beloved child in whom God as well pleased." (Matthew 3:17) God loves you and God is present in your life seeking to bring forth your love and, as a friend's T-shirt proclaims, there is nothing you can do about it. Claim the light in you. See the light in yourself and then be the light in others.

Building on the first chapter's spiritual practices, make a commitment, regardless of life's circumstances to be aware of your own Holiness, gaze upon the holiness of the world: of a child sleeping beside you, a prevaricating and ranting politician, an immigrant child, a companion animal, the wind in the trees, the cool morning air. While you may choose to vehemently oppose white Christian nationalism and politicians who manipulate the faithful to follow the wayward and divisive angels of their nature, still you can choose to see beyond their incivility, hate, and fear. You can feel your unity in God's ever-present love as an antidote to your own temptation to incivility and alienation.

A World of Praise. We are made for praise and thanksgiving. As Dag Hammarskjold (1905-1961) Secretary General of the United Nations from 1953-1961 affirmed,

> For all that has been – thanks!
> For all that shall be yes – yes!

Gratitude reflects the gift of graceful interdependence characterizing the Whiteheadian and Franciscan visions. Take time to give thanks and say thanks, to appreciate the gift of life, and the graces on your way.

Praise is the practice of honoring God's Creative Wisdom and Love moving through your life. A prayer I learned from the Shalem Institute of Spiritual Formation praises God with the words:

> I thank you God for the wonder of my being.
> I thank you God for the wonder of all being.

Rejoice in the wondrous grandeur and beauty of the universe and of your life. You are, as Psalm 139:14 proclaims, "fearfully [awesomely] and wonderfully made." Claim that radical amazement, as Abraham Joshua Heschel says, for yourself and for all creation.

If you come from a religious tradition which treasures hymns, you might praise God with your favorite hymns. Hymns of praise join you with God and all creation and contribute beauty to God's experience. The Great Empath rejoices in the unique gifts of love and praise that only you in your wild and precious uniqueness can contribute to the universe and God's experience. Some hymns that I treasure as inspiration to praise and comfort hymns are "Great is Thy Faithfulness" and "How Can I Keep from Singing." They are my mantras in times of struggle and despair.

> Great is thy faithfulness,
> Morning and evening new mercies I see,
> All that I've needed thy hand has provided,
> Great is thy faithfulness God unto me.[1]

> My life flows on in endless song
> amid earth's lamentation.
> I catch the sweet, though far off hymn,
> that hails a new creation.
> No storm can shake my inmost calm
> while to that rock I'm clinging.

---

[1] Thomas Chisholm, "Great is Thy Faithfulness." (1923)

> Since Love is lord of heaven and earth,
> How can I keep from singing?[2]

What hymns or songs, "sacred" or "secular," and the sacred is secular and the secular is sacred for Francis and Whitehead, speak to your soul's condition? What music, with or without words, evokes praise and gratitude? Let God's voice resound in your voice. Sing freely and joyfully and join the praises of all creation.

---

2   Robert Lowry (1869), "Pauline T" (1968), "How Can I Keep From Singing?"

3
WHITEHEAD AND CLARE

SEEING THE HUMBLE GOD

> O most Noble Queen, gaze upon [Christ],
> Consider [Christ],
> Contemplate [Christ],
> As you desire to imitate [Christ].³

> The life of Christ is not an exposition of over-ruling power…Its power lies in the absence of force. It has the decisiveness of a supreme ideal, and that is why the history of the world divides at this point in time.⁴

> When the Western world accepted Christianity, Caesar conquered…The brief Galilean vision of humility flickered throughout the ages, uncertainly. In the official formation of the religion, it has assumed the trivial form of the mere attribution of to the Jews that they cherished a misconception about their Messiah. But the deeper idolatry, of the fashioning of God in the image of the Egyptian, Persian, and Roman imperial rulers was retained. The

---

3 Regis Armstrong and Ignatius Brady, *Francis and Clare: The Complete Works* (Mahweh, NJ: Paulist Press, 1982), 183.
4 Whitehead, *Religion in the Making* (New York: Meridian, 1960), 56-57.

Church gave unto God the attributes which belonged exclusively to Caesar.[5]

Biblical scholar and theologian Terence Fretheim noted that it is more important to ask, "what kind of God do you believe in?" than "do you believe in God?" In that same spirit, Alfred North Whitehead noted that "a religion, on its doctrinal side, can thus be defined as a system of general truths which have the character of transforming character when they are sincerely held and vividly apprehended." The philosopher further noted that "in the long run your character of life depends upon your intimate convictions."[6]

What we believe about God, human life, and the non-human world really matters. Whitehead notes that religions are inherently ambiguous. They can inspire sacrifice and also provoke violence. In the United States and other nations, peoples' visions of God may even shape their politics and economics and response to climate change. I recall two encounters that provide graphic evidence of this. Recently, I engaged in a conversation with a fellow member of the Medicare generation, that is, USA retirees, at a local coffee shop. When he saw that I was reading a book on faith and the environment, he testified "I don't worry about climate change. Jesus is coming soon, the signs are everywhere, so what happens to the planet isn't important. In the meantime, my job is to save souls and provide for my family." Ironically, he went on to describe how well his retirement plans and investments were doing and how his future was financially secure. I was tempted to ask him, "If Jesus is coming soon, you won't need your retirement plans. Why don't you give me your investment portfolio so I can pay off my mortgage?"

---

5   Alfred North Whitehead, *Process and Reality: The Corrected Edition*, edited by David Ray Griffin and Donald Sherburne (New York: Free Press, 1978), 343.
6   Alfred North Whitehead, *Religion in the Making* (New York: Meridian, 1960), 15.

Another revealing encounter involved a conversation with a distant relative, a fundamentalist Christian whose faith is in an authoritarian omnipotent God who determines the course of history and the events of our lives. He confidently confided to me that "God is righteous and will destroy *his* foes, and in the meantime, we should do all we can to defeat them too – the liberals, woke, gays, Black Lives Matter, Antifa, and Democrat leaders such as Biden, Pelosi, and Harris. They're persecuting Christians. That's their goal, you know. They want to destroy Christianity and those who stand for family values. You can see it in how they are treating Trump, who's trying to save Christianity. God will prevail and destroy all *his* enemies, like *he* did at Sodom and Gomorrah!" I was aghast. He was describing me as one of God's "enemies," either knowingly or unknowingly. Perhaps, he was trying to pick a fight or put the fear of God in my heart and thought he was doing me a favor by giving me the opportunity to repent my universalism, thus saving me from God's wrath. At that moment, I kept my peace and as quickly as possible excused myself, obviously one of the anti-God crowd and bound for damnation, from his company.

Authoritarian gods and binary understandings of revelation lead to authoritarian politics and patriarchal and paternalistic relationships. The all-controlling Sovereign God encourages the divine right of kings, anti-democratic politicians, dominating superior-inferior relationships, destruction of indigenous peoples, homophobia, and male domination. Authoritarian, binary, violent images of God also encourage the conflation of God with our political heroes and the assumption that God blesses our politics and national agenda and rejects those with whom we disagree. As a sign during the insurrection of January 6, 2021, announced, "Jesus is my Savior. Trump is my president" as if the two statements are interchangeable. Following Donald Trump's felony conviction, many of his Christian followers posted memes on social media such as, "My savior was convicted, too!" or "The man I worship was convicted, too" as if Trump and Jesus are somehow both divinely chosen and that like Jesus, Trump is being martyred to bring salvation to the United States. Continuing the authoritarian tide, following the assassination attempt on Trump, many clearly asserted that his survival was due to God's diverting of the bullet, clear proof that he was God's chosen leader. In contrast, relational images of God and universalist understandings of revelation encourage diversity, democracy, and mutuality. God's love and inspiration are open to everyone and everyone, regardless of ethnicity, gender, sexual identity, or politics, deserves justice and respect.

In contrast to the limited and exceptionalist view of revelation and salvation, privileged by conservative Christianity, Whitehead, Francis, Clare, and Bonaventure proclaim a democracy of revelation which transcends religious traditions and cultures and sees something of God in everyone. If God embraces everyone, so should we, even when we challenge their positions and policies. If God's revelation touches everyone, we should treat everyone as a beloved child of God even when we have to protest the injustice they perpetrate. God loves the college student protesting the bombing of Gaza, the Zionist crusading for Israeli security, the MAGA Christian, and the progressive activist. Everyone has the potential to gaze upon and imitate Christ.

In this chapter, I will focus primarily on the relationship of Alfred North Whitehead and Clare of Assisi and their focus on the Galilean vision of Christianity, the loving and suffering Jesus, and their counsel to let the vision of a relational and intimate God guide our personal and political relationships. As we gaze upon the relational and loving God, our goal is to imitate the God we visualize and become persons of stature and compassion whose healing love includes all creation.

GAZING AT JESUS WITH CLARE

Clare of Assisi is a remarkable person of faith, who let go of power and privilege to embrace Holy Poverty and follow the Empathetic Christ. Clare and Francis met when Clare was in her teens and Francis his late twenties. Like Francis, Clare Offreduccio (1193-1253) was a child of wealth. But, more importantly, she was a child of divine destiny. Though her life course was not predetermined, the circumstances of her birth are an affirmation that God is revealed everywhere including the lives of fetuses and their mothers. This is not a political statement about the ethics of abortion or spiritual status of fetuses, but a recognition that God is alive and inspires our cells and souls, whether those of a fully grown woman deserving of the right to make decisions about her emotional and physical well-being or a fetus in the process of growth. During her pregnancy, Clare's mother was worried about her child's survival. Deeply spiritual, she prayed that God would bless her with a healthy child and received divine assurance that God would be with her, protecting her unborn child and prophesying that she would be a light to the world. In response, she chose the name "Chiara," or clear or luminous, for daughter. Clare lived up to the prophecy in her embodiment of clarity of mind and purity of heart. She became Francis' most luminous apostle.

Often overshadowed by both Francis and Bonaventure, Clare also inherited the economic, educational, social, and recreational advantages rarely available to the majority of young persons in her time. According to her biographers, she also was blessed with intelligence and beauty. Initially, her future was planned for her: social custom and the economic upward mobility prized by her class declared that she would marry into an affluent family like her own and live comfortably, carrying forward her husband's family line. Like Francis, Clare saw an alternative future ahead of her and sought another kind of family than the one planned for her.

Inclined toward the Spirit, while other girls and youth played with toys, admired dresses, and dreamed of marriage, Clare dedicated much of her childhood and youth to prayerful contemplation. Although many wealthy nobles sought her hand in marriage, she declared that she was looking for a very different kind of suitor, a Companion who would truly fulfill her spiritual desires.

She found her human spiritual companion in Francis and her Divine Companion in Jesus the incarnate and crucified one.

When Clare first heard Francis speak, the teenage spiritual seeker discovered that her quest could be fulfilled in a life of faithful simplicity, devoted fully to God. A spark ignited between the noble Clare and itinerant Francis, twelve years her senior, whose life story was similar to her own. Francis became her spiritual teacher, and she became, in her own words, his "little spiritual plant." But, Clare was far more than just Francis' protégé. The faithful and teachable plant grew into a mighty and fruitful tree. Initially inspired by Francis, Clare became her own person in a paternalistic society. Clare experienced the call to spiritual adventure, to embody women's spirituality, reflect the image of God in her life, and bring forth awareness of God's image in the lives of women – and men -whose lives she touched.

On Palm Sunday 1212, despite her family's strong objections, Clare abandoned privilege to become a follower of the One who inspired her spiritual guide Francis, the humble and empathetic Jesus the Christ. While Francis was initially Clare's spiritual mentor, Clare eventually found her own voice and path. She envisioned and then initiated a women's monastic order, complementary to the Franciscan brotherhood. Contrary to custom, Clare and her companions sought to create the Rule or practices they would follow as monastics rather than let them be dictated by male prelates. Though tethered to one spot due to spiritual convention and safety, the Poor Ladies or Poor Clares created a monastery at San Damiano, the church Francis repaired. Under her leadership, San Damiano became a place of hospitality for pilgrims, persons with leprosy, and the homeless and hungry. At San Damiano, Clare created her own structures of spiritual transformation, awakening women of all times and places, including our own, to their calling as God's beloved daughters, fully bearing the image of God, and not second class, as they were known in Clare's time, "occasions of sin," inferior to their male counterparts. One biographer of

Clare notes that "she succeeded in becoming holy in spite of being a woman."[7]

Clare evolved from being a student to an equal and perhaps Francis' closest spiritual friend. When Francis was seeking direction for the future of his ministry, he consulted Clare and followed her guidance. Legend has it that Francis and Clare were so spiritually close that one afternoon when the two met, observers believed a fire had broken out in the forest. The flames reflected their spiritually passionate love for each other. Claiming her identity and authority, Clare refused to have the rules of her Order written by a male and eventually received permission to author the Rules of the Poor Sisters. Clare felt God's inspiring and healing touch guiding her life and, despite the realities of patriarchy and hierarchy, asserted her call to spiritual leadership in the all-inclusive democracy of Spirit, described by Whitehead and embodied by Jesus and Francis.

Gazing at Jesus. The incarnate and embodied Christ is at the heart of Franciscan spirituality. The word made flesh, revealed in his miracles, teachings, cross, and resurrection, Christ, or Jesus, is our companion, guide, challenger, and model. Christ also is the embodied one, embracing the joys and sorrows of our world. Clare's spirituality centers on gazing at the crucified Christ as the embodiment of God's suffering love and the model of spiritual humility and simplicity. In focusing on Christ, literally seeing Christ as our closest companion and spiritual model, we commit ourselves to living in accordance with Christ's "rule" of love.

Many progressive Christians struggle with the meaning of the cross of Jesus and the necessity of his suffering for our salvation. Progressive Christians rightly critique atonement theories that focus on the necessity of Jesus' death on the cross as a preordained sacrifice to appease an angry God, pay an infinite debt to liberate us from finite sin, or model passive suffering as the highest virtue. They rightly note that for an Infinite and All-Loving God,

---

[7] Marco Bartoli, *Saint Clare: Beyond the Legend* (Cincinnati: Franciscan Media, 2010), 26.

there is no need for the appeasement or punishment of Jesus to secure our salvation. In contrast to violent and vengeful images of God, a Loving God, like a loving parent, embraces us in our imperfection and provides pathways for our healing. While Clare doesn't provide a theology of atonement, she believes that the Crucified Christ reveals the heart of God as empathetic love. When Jesus suffers, God also suffers. Jesus feels the pain of death, victimization, and injustice. The Parent of Jesus doesn't require our death. Jesus willingly dies to bring our healing and reconcile us with a God who already loves us. God loved us before the cross, God loved us on the cross, and God loves us in the unfolding of post-resurrection history.

God is not aloof or apathetic. God is embedded in the pain and joy of the world. God experiences our pleasure and pain and invites us to identify with and respond to the pain of the least of these: a child starving in sub-Sahara Africa, a young adult experiencing violence in the United States, a Ukrainian mother worried about her child in the military, a worm crushed by errant footstep, a transgender person ostracized by authoritarian Christians, and a wolf hunted by frightened villagers. God is known by God's emotional empathy not God's distant perfection. When we gaze upon the crucified Jesus, we experience the Sacred Heart of God, reflected in the love that brought Jesus to the cross, and in contrast to the emotional distance of an absent, apathetic, and punitive parent.

Holistic in spirit, Clare joined theological reflection and spiritual practice. When Clare counseled royal Agnes of Prague to gaze upon the cross, she sought to enable the noble woman to identify with Jesus' pain and the pain of the world. Gazing on the empathetic Jesus leads to contemplating God's love for us and then becoming Christ-like in our empathy with the pain of others. Salvation is found through the power of empathetic love and not the emotional apathy inherent in the love of power, whether that power is political or ecclesiastical. The relational God feels our pain, seeks our healing, and challenges us to feel the pain of others as the catalyst for our ministries of personal and social healing. In contrast to the empathetic and intimate God of Francis, Clare, Bonaventure, and Whitehead, the authoritarian apathetic God discourages empathy and sacrifice, and creates spiritual chasms between the saved and unsaved and orthodox and infidel.

The Incarnate Jesus is, to elaborate on a quote from Plato, the living or moving image of eternity. The eternal God is the most moved mover, and not the unmoved mover. God's glory is found in God's saving love for all creation. When we align our hearts with God's heart, as Clare counsels, we hear the heartbeat of God in the beating of our own hearts. Clare joins theology and spirituality in her counsel to her spiritual community.

> Place your mind before the mirror of eternity!
> Place your soul in the soul in the brilliance of glory!
> Place your heart in the figure of divine substance.
> And transform your whole being into
> the image of Godhead Itself through contemplation.[8]

When we allow our mind to be shaped by God's mind, we experience the glory of loving relationships and claim our divine image as God's beloved children. We come to embody the mind of Christ, described by the apostle Paul, in our humble identification with joys and sorrows of all creation.

> Let the same mind be in you that was in Christ Jesus,
> who, though he existed in the form of God,
>   did not regard equality with God
>   as something to be grasped,
> but emptied himself,
>   taking the form of a slave,
>   assuming human likeness.
> And being found in appearance as a human,
>   he humbled himself

---

8   Regis J. Armstrong and Ignatius C. Brady, *Francis and Clare: The Complete Works* (Mahweh, NJ: Paulist Press, 1982), 200.

and became obedient to the point of death—
even death on a cross. (Philippians 2:5-8)

To Paul's first century listeners, Clare's thirteenth century listeners, and today's twenty-first century followers of Jesus, the power of divine love and empathy embodied in Jesus contrasts with the unfeeling love of power exhibited in today's political dictators and ruthless politicians. While followers of Caesar throughout the ages rule by intimidation, retribution, and alienation, followers of the crucified Christ guide governments and religious traditions by affirmation, forgiveness, and healing. In embodying the mind of Christ, aligned with the Galilean origins of Christianity, we join our Savior and Guide in boundless compassion, inclusion, and hospitality.

The Spirit of Simplicity. The Shakers asserted that it is a gift to be simple and a gift to be free! Centuries before Ann Lee's mystical revelations that gave birth to the Shaker movement, Clare saw simplicity as the pathway to God awareness. Too often we are so encumbered by our lifestyles, busyness, and possessions that we are unable to experience the wonder of the present moment and the amazing reality of life within us and around us. When Clare speaks of poverty, her focus is pruning away everything that stands in the way of the Empathic and Suffering Christ and our vocation to be Christ's empathetic and healing companions. Holy Poverty refers not only to material possessions but also to doctrinal certainties, prejudices, attitudes, and behaviors that stand between us, our neighbor, and God. Francis let go of privilege to embrace the world in its entirety. No longer burdened by self-interest, prestige, possession, and the love of power, Francis and Clare saw God's presence in everyone and came to view every creature from the wolf of Gubbio to a lowly worm and a powerful Muslim sultan and an outcast person with leprosy as God's beloved children. Clare's hymn to Holy Poverty invites us to prune the inessential and unfruitful branches to let God's light shine brightly in our lives.

> O Holy Poverty, who bestows eternal riches on those who love and embrace her. O Holy Poverty, to those who possess and desire you God promises the kingdom of heaven and offers, indeed, eternal glory and blessed life. O God-centered poverty, whom the Lord Jesus Christ Who ruled and now rules heaven and earth, Who spoke and things were made, Who condescended to embrace before all else.[9]

In simplifying our lives, we make room for the ongoing revelations of the Risen Christ in our lives. The relational and all-Loving Christ is alive and lives within us, calling us to join Christ as God's companions in healing the world.

WHITEHEAD'S GALILEAN VISION

The impact of the life of Jesus on Whitehead's metaphysical vision is seldom addressed by theological and philosophical commentators. In his exploration of the Western intellectual and ethical adventure, Whitehead notes two critical moments in the progress of Western philosophy, religion, and civilization, still yet to be realized but constantly challenging us to wider horizons of ethics, politics, and theology. The first moment is found in the philosopher Plato's affirmation that "the divine element in the world is to be perceived as a persuasive agency and not as a coercive agency." According to Whitehead, Plato's vision of the interplay of divine and creaturely power is "one of the greatest intellectual discoveries in the history of religion." Whitehead adds that "the second phase is the supreme moment in religious history, according to Christianity. The essence of Christianity is the appeal to the life of Christ and his agency in the world."[10] Christian theology, at its best, and I believe Whitehead's theological reflections in particular, attempt to formulate a world view reflective of the Jesus' life, focusing on the power of love rather than the love of power and divine influ-

---
9   *Ibid.,* 192.
10 Whitehead, *Adventures in ideas* (New York: Free Press, 1933), 166-167.

ence by persuasion not coercion, to describe God's presence in our lives and the world. In many ways, the final chapter of *Process and Reality* is an essay in relational Christology in its focus on God as the Faithful Empath as well as the Universal Agent.

Process theologian Bernard Loomer, with whom I studied in my final year at Claremont Graduate School, spoke of two kinds of power: unilateral power and relational power. Unilateral power gives but never receives, condescends but never cooperates, mandates but never listens, compels but never partners. The "ideal" form of unilateral power is a divine or benevolent dictatorship, aimed at creating a perfect community through the interventions of one central and all-encompassing power source. By definition, even the highest and noblest forms of unilateral power, such as that envisioned in Plato's Republic are authoritarian, hierarchical, and coercive. The path toward the ideal faith or utopian community that idealistic ideologues seek is clear with no room for alteration. In contrast to the Platonic vision of wise authoritarianism, the epitome of unilateral power is found in the joining of divine omnipotence and divine determinism or predestination in which everything is ordered by God and any incursion of human agency, if that is even possible, is an affront to God. God decrees and we obey. The keys to salvation and damnation are entirely in God's hands. Every knee bows out of coercion and fear, whether to the tyrannical Caesar or the All-Sovereign God. To innovate or question is to go against God's ways. God is fully justified as Infinite Sovereign to mete out infinite damnation upon those who question God's authority, doubt "orthodoxy," or fail to meet God's standards.

This vision of authoritarian and coercive power undergirds the authoritarianism of human sovereigns. An authoritarian God has called authoritarian human leaders to rule over us. Chosen by God, these leaders have the divine right to be king or president regardless of the wisdom of their decision-making, competence, or election results. The authoritarian god mandates that his chosen ones civilize and bring God's culture to indigenous peoples and authorizes, since this God is often male, the superiority of men over women. Imitating the authoritarian and unilateral God, virtually every Western dictator or would-be USA populist political leader claims that God authorizes their use of power to marginalize, ostracize, and punish their foes. The authoritarian God inspires authoritarian leaders to be their "retribution," and their adoring followers become instruments of incivility and hate, all blessed by the God of Jesus Christ.

Process theologian Bernard Loomer suggests an alternative vision of God: the relational God embodied by Jesus, Clare, Francis, Bonaventure, and Whitehead. The relational God leads by mutuality and communication. The relational God listens as well inspires and adapts divine revelation to creaturely experience. Going beyond the binary, the relational God promotes a democracy of revelation in which each creature has the potential to reflect God's presence in its own unique way. When coercion, boundary setting, or consequences for inappropriate behavior need to be applied in a family or community, the goal of coercion is to cause as little suffering as possible and promote as much creativity and freedom congruent with community well-being. Relational visions of God inspire leadership that is relational in its quest for partners and not servants or slaves. Leaders and parents alike are mandated by a process-relational vision to be peacemakers, first, letting love define our boundaries and behaviors even in times of stress and duress.

Similar to Clare who sees the suffering love of Christ on the cross as the ultimate manifestation of divine relationship, Whitehead asserts that God is the fellow sufferer who understands. I believe that Whitehead would concur with Dietrich Bonhoeffer's assertion that only a suffering God can save us, a God who feels our pain, embraces our suffering, and seeks to soothe the pain of the world by providing healing possibilities in every situation. Whitehead's trinitarian vision of God complements Clare's understanding of the cross as the symbol of what Ilia Delio calls "the humility of God."[11]

Whitehead describes God in terms of the threefold and dynamic interdependence of the primordial, consequent, and superjective natures of God. In reality, these natures are intimately connected, and constantly evolving in relationship to one another and the world. None of the natures of God can exist and have agency apart from the others. When we focus on one aspect of Divinity in isolation to the others, we are engaging in necessary abstractions to help us the understand God's concrete relationship to the world in the same way that theologians speak of God as three persons and describe the inner trinitarian life of God (immanent Trinity) and the external historical activities of God (the economic Trinity). We cannot, however, mistake abstractions for the Living God. God is One, diverse, dynamic, interdependent, and constantly evolving and parents forth a diverse, dynamic, interdependent, and constantly evolving universe.

When Whitehead speaks of the primordial nature of God, he is referring the vast – if not infinite realm of possibility – nesting in the mind of God. These "eternal objects" are possibilities and potentials for any imaginable universe, planet, or situation. The teleology of the universe is aimed at the production of Beauty, the dynamic, complex, intense, and harmonious experience emerging in the course of cosmic, planetary, creaturely, and communal history. From the primordial nature, in the abstract, we have the first stirrings of the moral and spiritual arc of history and the positive energy of creativity. Without beginning or end, the primordial nature of God provides the framework of possibility for any imaginable universe.

God's consequent nature can be described as God's infinite, ongoing, and ever-evolving experience of the world. Within the consequent nature lie the "hopes and fears of all the years." God's love for the world embraces joy and sorrow, achievement and

---

11   Ilia Delio, *The Humility of God: A Franciscan Perspective* (Cincinnati: St. Anthony Messenger Press), 2005.

wreckage, and can be described as the tender care that nothing be lost. Our lives perish, moment by moment, and as a totality, but live evermore in God's ever-evolving embrace of the universe. The consequent nature of God is the suffering love of Christ, the fellow sufferer who understands, and the healing power of tragic beauty. When we empathetically gaze upon the universe and feel the pain of the vulnerable and forgotten as well as restless spirits of the privileged, our senses are fixed on the crucified and risen Jesus. Clare's vision of the suffering God is reflected in Whitehead's philosophical vision of God's consequent nature, the God who receives and empathizes and out of that Divine Empathy seeks our companionship in healing the world.

God's love flows back into the world as relevant possibility and the divine internal urge and energy to achieve God's vision as the superjective nature. Each moment emerges from the interplay of God and the world, from the creative synthesis of the historical matrix and previous decisions of each creature and divine possibilities urging that creaturely moment toward wholeness and beauty for itself and the world. According to Whitehead,

> [God's] purpose is always embodied in the particular ideals relevant to the actual state of the world. Thus all attainment is immortal in that it fashions the actual ideas which are God in the world as it is now. Every act leaves the world with a deeper or fainter impress of God. He then passes into his next relation to the world with enlarged, or diminished, presentation *of ideal values.*[12]

In all these dimensions of divine experience, God manifests a love that is patient, kind, and never ends. A love that inspires and does not control. An infinite love that evokes our highest possibilities and calls us to be God's companions in the wondrous adventure of global healing. A love, to paraphrase Thomas of Celano's description of Francis' spirituality, that is ever new, ever fresh, and always beginning again.

---

12 Whitehead, *Religion in the Making* , 152.

SPIRITUAL PRACTICES FOR GLOBAL HEALERS

Whitehead, Clare, Francis, and Bonaventure, proclaim a sensate theology, inviting us to experience God through sight as well as smell, touch, taste, and hearing, and paranormal and mystical experiences. The whole earth is full of God's glory. We can" taste and see" God's presence in the world. God is more than we can imagine and transcends our finite experience, as *apophatic* spirituality asserts. No words can fully describe God nor can we identify God fully with any particular religious experience or theological doctrine. God also comes to us revealing Godself through the five senses and heightened sense experience, characteristic of *kataphatic t*heology.

Gazing at the Empathetic Christ. Clare invites us to gaze at the life of Christ. Clare counsels us to see a moment in Christ's life as a reflection of God's love for you and the world and a pattern for you own life. Clare's counsel to Agnes of Prague is timeless and can transform our lives if we take it to heart and become one in Spirit with Jesus of Nazareth.

> Gaze upon [Christ],
> Consider [Christ],
> Contemplate [Christ],
> As you desire to imitate [Christ].

Find a particular moment in Christ's life upon which to focus. Fix your attention on the gospel narrative. Visualize Jesus' interactions with those around him. You may choose, in the spirit of Ignatius of Loyola to become one of the characters in the scene, even seeing yourself as Jesus. See yourself reflecting God's wise and suffering love. Let the scene unfold with you as one of the participants.

Ponder the meaning of the gospel story you have chosen for your life. What are learning about God's empathetic love and your call to embody that love in daily life and citizenship? What would it be like for you to "imitate" Christ's behavior and values in your personal, relational, professional, and political decision-making?

Conclude by considering ways you can integrate what you have learned about the empathic Christ in your daily life and relationships. What one thing can you do to be more in alignment with God's vision of personal and global empathy?

Here are some gospel stories from which you might choose in your quest to experience and embody God's Empathetic Love.

> Fellowship with sinners and tax collectors – Mark 2:13-17
> The storm at sea – Mark 4:35-41
> The woman with the flow of blood – Mark 5:25-34
> Jairus' daughter – Mark 5: 35-43
> Jesus blessing the children – Mark 10:13-16
> The encounter with Zaccheaus – Luke 19:1-10
> The woman caught in adultery – John 8:1-11
> Jesus' resurrection encounter with Mary of Magdala – John 20:11-18

Simplicity of the Spirit. According to Alfred North Whitehead, the world lives by the incarnation of God. As incarnate in the world, Christ is the principle of creative transformation, as John Cobb asserts. Everywhere and in all things, God seeks beauty, justice, wholeness, and fulfillment. Yet, God always comes to us within the totality of our experiences. God's aim at wholeness and Shalom emerge as one of the components of each moment of experience. Accordingly, to experience the divine aim, we need to pause, notice, and respond. This requires a type of holy simplicity in which we prune away everything that prevents us from experiencing God's vision for our lives. While there are many practices that awaken us to God's moment by moment vision, one spiritual practice that I have found helpful is simply to take time to listen to the divine voice moving within all the other voices we hear. In the spirit of the prophet Elijah, we might ask "Speak, God, your servant is listening." Then, breathe deeply opening to the currents of God's presence moving through your life. With the Jesuit spiritual guide Pierre de Caussade, such silence awakens us to the "sacrament of the present moment." In this fleeting divine moment, we may choose to ask questions such as "what would you have me do in this situation?," "what is my vocation in this setting?," or "how might I serve God and those around me?"

As we listen for God's presence, we may receive clear answers; synchronous events may awaken us to the path ahead; a dream or intuition may point us in the direction we need to take; or we persevere with patience and hope that a way toward the future will eventually emerge.

4

THE FOUNTAIN OF LOVE

BONAVENTURE AND WHITEHEAD

God within all things, but not enclosed;
outside all things, but not excluded;
above all things, but not aloof;
below all things, but not debased.
Finally, because it is supremely one and all-inclusive,
it is therefore,
all in all…
from him, in him, and through him are all things.[13]

The action of the fourth phase [of God's nature, according to Whitehead] is the love of God for the world. It is the particular providence for particular occasions. What is done in the world is transformed into a reality in heaven, and the reality in heaven passes back into the world. By reason of this reciprocal relation, the love in the world passes into the love in heaven and floods back into the world. In this sense, God is the great companion – the fellow sufferer who understands.[14]

---

13 Bonaventure, *The Soul's Journey into God, The Tree of Life, The Life of St. Francis,* translated by Ewert Cousins, (Mahweh, NJ: Paulist Press, 1978), 100-101.

14 Alfred North Whitehead, *Process and Reality: Corrected Edition.* Edited by David Ray Griffin and Donald Sherburne (New York: Free Press, 1979), 351.

Chapter Three's conversation between Alfred North Whitehead and Clare of Assisi emphasized divine receptivity. God is the Ultimate Empath, who lovingly embraces the world in all its complexity. Nothing is alien to God. No one outside the circle of God's love. The cross is the symbol of divine solidarity with creation. The most moved mover is moved by the world. The crucifixion of Jesus reveals the humility of God, the "fellow sufferer who understands" and the intimate companion who rejoices. As the ultimate expression of God's loving companionship, Jesus suffers and dies for our healing: not to appease an angry, thin skinned, and easily insulted and domineering God but to enable us to discover the depth of God's love and God's willingness to suffer that we might find wholeness. Like the shepherd seeking the hundredth sheep, the woman looking for a lost coin, or a parent running out, against social custom, humiliating themselves to embrace a wayward child (Luke 15), God's Empathy knows no boundaries. God is the most moved mover. The love that is finite in us is infinite in God. Even the gates of hell cannot deter divine love. God searches "until" every lost one is embraced in God's "consequent nature," God's "tender care is that nothing is lost."[15] For Clare and Whitehead, God is the heart of the universe. The most moved mover, as Abraham Joshua Heschel asserts, is truly moved by our feelings and touched by our struggles. God's humility is God's receptivity and willingness to be changed by the world. In contrast to the unilateral, judgmental, coercive, and authoritarian god who models retribution, domination, and emotional distancing found in politics and personal relationships, the relational and humble deity envisaged by Clare and Whitehead inspires partnership, egalitarian relationships, and empathy in political decision-making and personal relationships.

In this chapter, Whitehead dialogues with Bonaventure on God's world shaping activity. The most moved mover gives as well as receives and moves through all things shaping and guiding them in accordance with God's intimacy with the world. The mor-

---

15 Alfred North Whitehead, *Process and Reality*, 346.

al and spiritual arcs of history are present as the motive force every moment of experience and the long haul of human and planetary history. God joins activity and receptivity in God's quest to heal the Earth, and calls us to do likewise. God's power in the world is intimately connected with the world's impact on God.

Divine humility joins God's responsive and creative love. God's love is never abstract but responds concretely to every creature's situation in light of its environment, previous decisions, and God's aim is at the production of beauty in whole and part. Theologian Thomas Oord describes the power of this open and relational God in terms of the word "amipotence" in contrast to "omnipotence." God's non-coercive love is the ever-present companion working with the world rather than coercively determining the world. To use the language of Bonaventure, God's love is an ever-flowing stream of light and love giving birth to the universe and every moment of experience. God's energy of love, described by Whitehead and Bonaventure moves through all things and within all things adapting to their experiences and shaping their actions in light of God's loving vision of beauty and wholeness.

BONAVENTURE'S FOUNTAIN OF LOVE

Whitehead and Bonaventure were similar in many ways: they were professors, writers, and administrators. Their thought ranged from exploring the universe to considering the lilies of the field. They had a keen eye to history and tradition – Bonaventure wrote a biography of St. Francis and sought to reform Christian theology focusing on the dynamic movements of God in the world rather than the apathetic unmoved mover, characteristic of Thomas Aquinas' Aristotelian vision. Whitehead explored the history of Western civilization in *Adventures of Ideas*. Both recognized the power of ideas to transform our lives and the world.

John di Fidanza (1217-1274), who took the name Bonaventure when he became a Franciscan, has been called the second founder of the Franciscan Order. The son of a physician, Bonaventure, possessed an ecumenical vision that joined order and novelty and tradition and innovation. As Minister General of the Franciscan Order, he sought to unite the itinerant monks with their more stable academic companions. Later, he was asked by Pope Gregory X to seek a similar unity between the Roman and Greek branches of Christianity.

Francis shaped Bonaventure's life from childhood. As a child, Bonaventure was healed of a life threatening illness as result of his family's invocation of Francis' healing powers. In his biography of Francis, Bonaventure recalls, "When I was a boy, as I vividly remember, I was snatched from the jaws of death by his [Francis'] invocation and merits. So if I remained silent and did not sing his praises, I fear that I would be rightly accused of the crime of ingratitude. I recognize that God saved my life through him, and I realized that I have experienced his power in my very person."[16]

At age seventeen, Bonaventure began theological studies at the University of Paris, where he encountered Franciscans whose integration of mind, heart, and hands transformed his life and mission. Bonaventure entered the Franciscan Order as a result of his awe at the Christ-like spirit of Francis, whom he believed to be the ultimate embodiment of Jesus' ministry. While not inclined toward either itinerant wandering or dramatic mystical experiences, Bonaventure found his life transformed at Alverna, the site of Francis' mystical experience in which Francis embodied the stigmata of Jesus. Bonaventure's mystical alignment with Francis' experience became the inspiration of Bonaventure's classic on Franciscan and Western Christian spirituality, *The Soul's Journey to God*. In his own words, Bonaventure described this life-changing experience.

> While I was there [La Verna] reflecting on the various ways by which the soul ascends to God, there came to mind, among other things, the miracle which had occurred to blessed Francis in this very place: the winged Seraph in the form of the Crucified. While reflecting on this, I *saw at once* our

---
16 Ibid., 182.

father's rapture in contemplation and the road by which this rapture is reached.[17]

At La Verna, Bonaventure truly had a holistic experience of God, mediated through the intimacy of his encounter with Francis' own mystical experience. The mystical and intellectual were joined as Bonaventure experienced first-hand the ecstatic love of God that inspired Francis' ministry and enabled the saint of Assisi to see himself as Christ's companion in healing the world. Like Whitehead, Bonaventure joined mysticism and metaphysics in his dynamic vision of God's self-diffusing love. As I ponder the history of Christian theology, I wonder how Christianity might have evolved had the church privileged or equalized Bonaventure's vision of God as an ever-flowing world-affirming fountain of love rather than his Dominican contemporary Thomas Aquinas' (1225-1274) vision of God as unmoved mover, whose unchanging perfection, rendered God distant from and unaffected by the joys and sorrows of life. Together Bonaventure and Aquinas reflect the interplay of the ever-changing and the unchanging in God's nature, what Whitehead later was to describe as the consequent and primordial natures of God as the foundation for God's activity in the world.

The Fountain of Love. Bonaventure believed that the Divine Fountain of Love flows through all creation, giving birth to flora and fauna, the birds of the air, the fish of the sea, and humankind. Each human bears the divine image, and the ability to encounter God directly. The Divine Fountain flows through you and everything else, energizing each creature from the inside as well as outside, bringing life and love to you, and connecting you with the Crucified Christ. Despite our turning away from God's ever-flowing love and light through self-interest and greed, God still speaks to and through us. If we pause a moment, we can hear God's whisper and feel God's breath. We can feel God's wisdom <u>and creativity</u> flowing through us and welling up from within us.

---

[17] Bonaventure, *The Soul's Journey to God, The Tree of Life, The Life of St. Francis*, 54-55. (my italics)

Bonaventure invites us to "picture in your mind a tree whose roots are watered by an ever-flowing fountain that becomes a great and living river," reflecting "the power of salvation for everyone who believes." (Romans 1:6)[18] This "Fountain of life and light," nourishes the church and our spirits, mystics and seekers, and just as importantly nurtures all creation, human and non-human alike.

The flow, dare I say Tao, of God's ever-creative love is intimate, dynamic, life-giving, and global. Nothing is outside God's love nor is any creature alien from the One to whom all hearts are open and all desires known. Bonaventure describes God as:

> an intelligible sphere whose center is everywhere and whose circumference is nowhere."[19]

As our center, the heartbeat of God beats within our own hearts and the wisdom of God guides our steps, even when we are unaware or turn from God's vision. As the all-inclusive loving substance, God holds creation together. There is no outsider or alien. All things emerge from and are energized by the constantly flowing divine fountain. Nor, in contrast to Augustine and Calvin, is anyone lost or forsaken by the divine companion. Bonaventure's all-inclusive metaphysics of love gives shape to Francis' affirmation, "God and all things."

While Bonaventure recognizes that the spiritual quest, the soul's journey to God, requires focusing on the spirit as well as the senses and involves transcending the senses to experience the peaceful unity of God, Bonaventure rejoices, like Francis, in the beauty of the world. We live, as I noted earlier, in a world of praise in which deep down all things experience God and reveal God's wisdom and love. The world is a shrine and symphony, not a soul stifling prison or punishment for sin. On our journey to God, all things declare God's loving presence and remind us to seek divinity in the flow of time. The ever-changing and never-chang-

---

18 Bonaventure, *The Soul's Journey into God, The Tree of Life, and The Life of St. Francis,* 120.
19 Ibid.,100.

ing meet in each moment of experience and together urge us to self-transcending spiritual involvement in the world.

> We can contemplate God not only outside us and within us but also above us; outside through his vestiges, within through his images, and above through the light which shines upon our minds, which is the light of eternal truth.[20]

The heavens declare the glory of God. (Psalm 19:1) Our cells reveal God's aim at wholeness. Our spirit revels in the Breath of God. The wolf of Gubbio howls forth God's praises and so too does the laughter of a child and the chanting of a monk. Bonaventure declares that "whoever is not enlightened by such splendor of created things is blind." The Seraphic Doctor counsels us "open your eyes, alert the ears of your spirit, open your lips, and apply your heart so that in all creatures you may see, hear, praise, love and worship, glorify and honor your God."[21] Bonaventure would agree with Louis Armstrong's affirmation, "I say to myself, 'What a wonderful world.'" God is revealed in the: "magnitude of things," the grandeur of the world, which "manifests the immensity of the power, wisdom, and goodness of the triune God"; "the multitude of things," reflective of God's love for diversity and the constant interplay of unity and diversity; "the fullness of things" in their power and possibility; the vitality and "activity of things," revealing God's "power, art, and goodness"; the "order of things," seasons of seedtime and harvest, day and night, the revolutions of the heavens; and through it all, "the beauty of things in the variety, shape and color in simple, mixed, and even organic bodies – heavenly bodies and minerals (like stones and metals) and plants and animals." Bonaventure concludes his own hymn to God's loving creativity, flowing in and through all things with the counsel:

> Whoever therefore who is not enlightened
> by such splendor of created things

---

20   Bonaventure, *The Soul's Journey into God, The Tree of Life, The Life of St. Francis*, 94.
21   Ibid., 68.

is blind;
Whoever is not awakened by such outcries
is deaf;
Whoever does not praise God because of all of these effects
is dumb;
Whoever does not discover the First Principle
from such clear signs is a fool.
Therefore, open your eyes,
alert the ears of your spirit, open your lips
and apply your heart
so that in all creatures you may
see, hear, praise, love, worship, glorify and honor
your God.[22]

We live in a God-filled world, in which God breathes through, energizes, and guides all things, without determining all things. As the hymn proclaims, "all nature sings and around me rings the music of the spheres."[23] While Bonaventure does not explore the question of the extent of divine power, he rejoices in the fecundity, beauty, creativity, and agency of the world as it reflects and imitates the fecundity, beauty, creativity, and agency of God.

Following his spiritual mentor Francis in his intimacy with the non-human world and hymns to creation, Bonaventure invites us to treasure both the human and non-human world. God's life-giving fountain of love nourishes every creature and that is our calling as well, to be healers of the earth. God's love for the world inspires our love for God's world. We don't have to choose between loving God and the world. As we spiritually ascend to the heavens, moving from the many to the One, we also move from the One to the many: we love the Creator by loving God's creatures. We love the creatures rightly when we place God first as the ever-present center of our lives and our relationships, recognizing that all things dwell in the circle of God's love. Mystical experiences broaden and deepen our experience, and join the eternal

---
22 Ibid, 65-68.
23 Maltbie D. Babcock, "This is My Father's World." (1901).

and temporal, rather than inspiring us to abandon the diverse and perpetual perishing world of daily life.

Patterns of Divine Presence. Bonaventure imagines God's nature and presence in the world in terms of "emanation, exemplarity, and consummation." While these are words that seldom appear in today's everyday language and scholarly writing, they reveal Bonaventure's vision of the patterns of divine creativity and presence in the world. "Emanation" or "dynamic Creative Wisdom" describes God's constant process of bringing forth the universe from the beginning of time to this present moment. Bonaventure marveled at God's creative word (*logos, dabhar*), described in the biblical creation stories, calling forth the sun, stars, and sea, the creatures of flight, foot, and fin, and finally humankind in its diversity as the image of the triune God. God is still speaking, and God is still creating, and although Bonaventure sees humankind as the crown of creation, there are vestiges of divinity in all things. God is present in all things and thus all things share in God's beauty, wisdom, goodness, artistry, and power. Holiness is everywhere and not reserved for humankind. In reflecting God's Emanating Power and Presence in experiences of love and unity, we also emanate and diffuse our agency into the world.

"Exemplarity" refers to the "Mind of God," or what Whitehead calls the "Primordial Nature of God," and to the divine pattern, inspiring, energizing, and organizing all creation. A reflection of Divine Wisdom and Intelligence, creation is the book of divine creativity, and all things are words of God and revelations of the Divine Word who brings forth all things. God has patterned the universe and human life, body, mind, and spirit, to remind us of our Creator and our inner divinity and inspire us to fulfill our destiny as God's beloved children. Exemplarity is the embodiment of the divine order that promotes creativity, and the pattern that inspires the spiritual quest. In the spirit of Psalm 8, we marvel at God's infinite creativity, recognize our finitude in the vastness of the universe, and in response to the mysticism of infinity, claim our role as God's agents in caring for creation. The world is not random and purposeless. The world is created by God that we might live in harmony with one another and creation and seek to align our spirits with God's Spirit. While the Mind of God is imperfectly realized in the perpetually perishing of our lives and in the vestiges of the non-human world, as reflections of the Divine Mind, we are agents of creativity and healing able to do something beautiful in response to the Source of All Beauty.

Broadly speaking, "emanation" and "exemplarity" describe the origins of the universe, human and non-human existence, and the rising of each unique moment, while "consummation" refers to what Whitehead describes as the "teleology of the universe" aiming at beauty and Teilhard calls the Christ Omega or Christogenesis. While intimately connected with emanation and exemplarity, consummation describes the aim of life and vision of God for us. God's ever-flowing fountain of love will be recognized by all creation. God will be, as the apostle Paul proclaims, "all in all." The imperfection and conflict of history and our personal lives is neither the pattern nor goal of life but a fall from grace due to human waywardness and the accidents of life. Still even our waywardness reflects the presence of the creative and loving God, whose aim is always peace and wholeness.

In many ways, Bonaventure's vision of consummation reflects what nineteenth century Unitarian minister and abolitionist Theodore Parker described as the "moral arc of history," what I have expanded to "the moral and spiritual arcs history". While we can stall the realization of God's dream for history and human life, God is the Alpha and Omega, and the beginning and goal of life, the spiritual and moral arcs of history, will eventually be realized on earth as it is in heaven. The image of God, the fully alive human, hidden from us by individual and institutional sin and injustice will be restored in us and all humankind. All things will recognize the divine center in themselves and embrace the circle whose circumference is nowhere in its embrace of creation in all its wondrous diversity.

> God within all things, but not enclosed;
> outside all things, but not excluded;
> above all things, but not aloof;
> below all things, but not debased.
> Finally, because it is supremely one and all-inclusive,
> it is therefore,
> all in all…
> from him, in him, and through him are all things.[1]

It would be remiss in talking about God's action in the universe to omit Bonaventure's vision of God's humility. Ilia Delio describes Bonaventure's vision of divine creative-receptive relationality: "God's power is in his humility, God's strength is in his weakness, God's greatness is in his lowliness."[2] In God's solidarity with us, God is:

> The first, the last,
> The highest and the lowest,
> The circumference and the center,
> The Alpha and Omega,
> The cause and the caused,
> The Creator and creature.[3]

The within and without of all things, God does not coerce but inspires. God's creativity is God's receptivity, God's eternity is God's temporality, God's greatness is in service and solidarity.

---

1 Ibid., 100-101.
2 Ilia Delio, *The Humility of God: A Franciscan Perspective* (Cincinnati: St. Anthony Messenger, 2005), 83. Quoting Ewart Cousins, *Bonaventure*, 107.
3 *Bonaventure, The Soul's Journey into God, The Tree of Life, The Life of St. Francis,* 108-109.

WHITEHEAD'S INSPIRATIONAL AND ADVENTUROUS GOD

A major theme of this text is what Ilia Delio describes as the "humility of God." In contrast to authoritarian, domineering, coercive, and binary gods, who provoke similar behaviors among their followers in their personal and political lives, Francis, Clare, Bonaventure, and Whitehead affirm a relational, persuasive, invitational, and all-embracing deity. While God has definite purposes in history – the moral and spiritual arcs aim toward justice and beauty– God guides the universe at the micro and macro levels, by the power of love, sacrifice, and companionship. When we gaze upon Jesus as the mirror of God's character, we are inspired, to use Clare's language, to imitate the all-loving and all-embracing God in our citizenship and relationships. Just as God is "the circle (or infinite sphere) whose center is everywhere and whose circumference is nowhere," we are called to see God's presence in each creature and recognize that within the circle of love there are no outsiders, and act accordingly. While there may be occasions for challenge, discipline, and boundary-making, these divine and human actions are motivated by the quest for wholeness, healing, and justice, and not control or dominance.

As an apostle of the humility of God, Whitehead asserted that God rules by the power of the ideal. While the worship of God may inspire prophetic protest and caring confrontation, the aim is healing and the realization of God's all-inclusive aim at beauty in our personal relationships and citizenship. Whitehead's dynamic and relational God is uniquely triune in Godself and relationship to the world. This is not the trinity of traditional Creedal Christianity but the intimate and dynamic trinitarian vision of God's presence in the world, described by the primordial, consequent, and superjective natures of God. As we talk about these three natures, we must – as we do with Creedal Christianity, at its best – remember that they are one, interdependent, dynamic, and interactive. Just as God and the world exist in dynamic relationship, without beginning and end, the natures of God reveal diversity and relationality in the oneness of God. Apart from the others, any of God's "natures" is an abstraction. The living God is the wealth of possibility and ideals, the heart of the universe, infinite and ever-evolving memory, and companion of creation, and the moral, spiritual, and artistic vision relevant to each moment of experience. Together, they bring forth an evolving world of praise in which each creature is a "word of God," energized and inspired by God's fountain of love.

In the dialogue of Clare and Whitehead, I emphasized the consequent nature of God as revelatory of the affirmation that God is the fellow sufferer who understands. As the Empathetic Heart of the Universe, God feels the pain and joy of the world. God feels the anxiety of Israeli and Gazan parents, the anger of Black Lives Matter protesters, the fear of MAGA supporters, and the uneasiness of those who see ominous images of their children's future placarded in daily weather reports. God's consequent nature is the tender care that nothing is lost. God's empathetic love inspires our prayers and sense that we are not alone. Jesus is our companion in joy and sorrow. We are born into loving arms and will be received at death into loving arms. Nothing can separate us from the love of God. (Romans 8:38-39) Even if our quest to heal the Earth fails, our efforts are treasured forever in God's consequent nature.

God's primordial nature is the unbounded realm of possibility. God is infinitely and eternally resourceful. God's power in in God's infinite imagination and ability to energize and inspire the world with ideals. As primordial, God creates the framework of any possible universe through God's vision of the infinity of possibility, described as the realm of eternal objects residing in the mind of God. Just as there has never been the world apart from God and God apart from the world, there has always been a realm of eternal objects as characteristic of God's nature and irrelevant apart from God's evolving agency.

God imagines a world. God experiences a world. And God shapes a world. I identify God's action in the world as related to and grounded in God's receptive consequent nature, the moment by moment and creature by creature joining of the ideal and possible, revealing to each moment of experience and, I believe, each community the "best for that impasse," based on context, environment, previous decisions, and future hopes. God embraces the world, feeling its wondrous and diverse joy and sorrow, and guided by God's vision "incarnates" Godself in our lives and world.

God's consequent nature finds its active and embodied expression in what Whitehead describes the superjective nature of God explicitly only once in *Process and Reality:* "The 'superjective' nature of God is the character of the pragmatic value of his specific satisfaction qualifying the transcendent creativity in the various temporal instances" (PR 135). Just as the consequent nature can be described by the second couplet of the pantheistic credo: "all things in God," the superjective nature can be characterized by the first line of the credo: "God in all things" as the immanence, incarnation, and inspiration of God in the world. Two passages from Whitehead describe God's non-coercive and humble presence in the world:

> The perfected actuality [God's satisfaction] passes back into the temporal world, and qualifies this world so that each temporal actuality includes it as an immediate fact of relevant experience.[4]
>
> [The love of God for the world] is the particular providence for particular occasions. What is done in the world is transformed into a reality in heaven, and the reality in heaven passes back into the world. By reason of this reciprocal relation, the love in the world passes into the love in heaven and floods back into the world. [God's] purpose is always embodied in the particular ideals relevant to the actual state of the world. Thus all attainment is immortal in that it fashions the actual ideas which are God in the world as it is now. Every act leaves the world with a deeper or fainter impress of God. He

---

4   Whitehead, *Process and Reality,* 351.

then passes into his next relation to the world with enlarged, or diminished, presentation of ideal values.[5]

God is both the restless spirit and foundation of order in our lives and the universe. The Ultimate Empath, God is also the Universal Source of Inspiration. God calls humankind forward toward the embodiment of Shalom, beauty, and justice. God also undergirds the call to creative transformation with regularity, predictability, and constancy, described by the authors of Lamentations 3:22:

> The steadfast love of the LORD never ceases,
>   his mercies never come to an end;
> they are new every morning;
>   great is your faithfulness.

God's love never ends. God is faithful in every season of life. As source of possibility and empathetic companion, God is always with us, sustaining and challenging. As source of novelty and challenge, God inspires us and our institutions toward the far horizons of justice and hospitality, and to the realization of a world in which "justice rolls down like waters and righteousness like an ever-flowing stream." (Amos 5:24) God's power is evolving, all-embracing, and unlimited in that God shapes every moment of creation. Every center is touched by God's moment by moment initial aim, relevant to its world, experience, and choices. God's aim is always intimate and personal, contextual and communal, and never domineering. God's prophetic presence makes demands, but these demands are congruent with our world and our experience. As "amnipotent," love, described by Thomas Jay Oord, God moves through all things and finds its joy in the expansion of freedom and creativity for all and not domination and constraint. God evolves along with the world. A living God is a changing God, both in God's experience and God's activity. In contrast to the Living, Relational, and Evolving God, the Au-

---

5   Whitehead, *Religion in the Making.*, 152.

thoritarian and Unchanging God who predestines and chooses all things is confined in a strait jacket by God's own eternal decisions, is unable to innovate, and is the source of suffering as well as joy, damnation as well as salvation. For the authoritarian God, God's best days are in the past; for the Innovative and Relational God, this moment is a holy moment, giving birth to the open horizons of tomorrow. Only the humble, uncontrolling, all-loving, and all-healing God of Whitehead and the parents of Franciscan spirituality can provide the vision and inspiration we need to heal the world in companionship and imitation of the Ultimate Empath, Visionary Challenger, and Horizon of Possibility. The humble relational God is constantly growing with and going into the world, blending fact and vision, in the quest for Shalom. The intimate non-coercive God guides the universe by persuasion and models persuasive leadership in congregational leadership, economics and business, politics, and parenting and interpersonal relationships.

SPIRITUAL PRACTICES FOR GLOBAL HEALERS

Bonaventure visualizes God as a fountain of love and light flowing through you and all creatures. The flow of love comes from beyond as well as within, inspiring and energizing each moment of experience. Whitehead sees God's power as inspirational and persuasive. God provides a moment-by-moment vision of what we – and all creation – can become. Whitehead describes God's vision as invitational and not coercive. God motivates, inspires, and empowers. In similar fashion, when we go with the flow of God's fountain love, our agency and freedom expand. Divine energy awakens us to our own energy and when we are attentive energizes us in novel, creative, and expansive ways.

Going with the Flow of God's Love. Over the years, I have heard the popular counsel "go with the flow," as a way of surrendering the currents of life. Rather than being passive, going with the flow can be described in a short form of the Serenity Prayer, written by theologian Reinhold Niebuhr:

> God grant me the serenity to accept
> the things I cannot change;
> Courage to change the things I can;
> And the wisdom to know the difference.

Recently, a line penned by Angela Davis was added in activist circles, "Change what I cannot accept."

In this exercise, visualize God's flowing fountain of light and love flowing in and through you with every breath and movement. Align yourself with the Tao of Divine Creativity. Feel God's ever-flowing streams of life carrying you forward. Let the ripples of divine love propel and guide you as you ask for guidance, "Let my life be an ever-flowing stream of love and healing as the waters of your fountain of love and light flow in and through me to everyone I meet. Show me the way to let your stream of love flow in ways that bring healing to the earth and those around me."

Awakening to Beauty. Bonaventure and Whitehead are philosophers of beauty, who invite us to live in a world of enchantment and praise. For Whitehead, the teleology of the universe is aimed at the production of beauty, complexity and intensity of experience. This is both a personal and political issue. We are challenged to create societies that promote beauty of experience through ensuring education, leisure, sustenance, and healthcare for all citizens. For Bonaventure, the beauty of the world reflects and points us to God's beauty. Beautiful environments and the opportunity to create beauty are spiritual requirements for full humanity and openness to divinity. We embrace beauty one moment at a time and discover from these first glimpses of beauty, a beautiful world becomes our daily experience and gift to others. As Bonaventure counsels:

> Therefore, open your eyes,
> alert the ears of your spirit, open your lips
> and apply your heart

so that in all creatures you may
see, hear, praise, love, worship, glorify and honor
your God.⁶

In this practice, I invite you to take what process theologian and author Patricia Adams Farmer describes as a "beauty break." I cite her work in virtually every book I've written as an inspiration to living in the Holy Here and Now. Awaken to God's beautiful world through meditating on Gerard Manley Hopkins, "Pied Beauty."

The poet-priest Hopkin's "Pied Beauty" has a personal meaning for me. Theologian, dear friend, and at the time fellow graduate student Catherine Keller read Hopkins' "Pied Beauty" and "God's Grandeur" at Kate's and my wedding at the Claremont Colleges Chapel in January 1979. Take time to read and reflect on this poem and then ponder the many faces of beauty as you go through the day.

> Glory be to God for dappled things –
>   For skies of couple-colour as a brindled cow;
>   For rose-moles all in stipple upon trout that swim;
> Fresh-firecoal chestnut-falls; finches' wings;
>   Landscape plotted and pieced – fold, fallow, and plough;
>   nd áll trádes, their gear and tackle and trim.
>
> All things counter, original, spare, strange;
>   Whatever is fickle, freckled (who knows how?)
>   With swift, slow; sweet, sour; adazzle, dim;
> He fathers-forth whose beauty is past change:
>   Praise him.

As a walker and hiker, I have always appreciated the Navajo Blessing Way and its hymn to beauty. If you are able, take time to read this poem and then go on a walk. Take a "saunter," or walk in a holy way or the holy land of each step you take, as American

---

6 Bonaventure, *The Soul's Journey into God, The Tree of Life, The Life of St. Francis*, 65-68.

Transcendentalist Henry David Thoreau counsels. In the spirit of the North African monks' comment that the "monk is all eye," feast your eyes on beauty and vow to be a beauty-seeker and beauty-maker. In the politics of beauty, vow to make the world a more beautiful place by your actions and citizenship. Make a commitment to challenge anything that stands in the way of persons experiencing beauty and advocate for the creation of structures of beauty as you meditate on the Navajo (Dine) blessing.

> Beauty in front of me, Beauty behind me,
> Beauty Above me, Beauty below me,
> Beauty all around me,
> I walk in Beauty…..
> In the house of long life, there I wander.
> In the house of happiness, there I wander.
> Beauty before me,
> Beauty behind me,
> Beauty above me ,
> Beauty below me,
> Beauty all around me,
> In old age traveling, with it I wander.
> On the beautiful trail I am, with it I wander.
> In beauty, it is begun,
> In beauty, it is finished.

5
HEALING THE PLANET

THE QUEST FOR ECOLOGICAL CIVILIZATION

*Be praised, my Lord, through all your creatures,
especially through my lord Brother Sun,
who brings the day; and you give light through him.
And he is beautiful and radiant in all his splendor!
Of you, Most High, he bears the likeness.*

*Praise be You, my Lord, through Sister Moon
and the stars, in heaven you formed them
clear and precious and beautiful.*

*Praised be You, my Lord, through Brother Wind,
and through the air, cloudy and serene,
and every kind of weather through which
You give sustenance to Your creatures.*

*Praised be You, my Lord, through Sister Water,
which is very useful and humble and precious and chaste.*

*Praised be You, my Lord, through Brother Fire,
through whom you light the night and he is beautiful
and playful and robust and strong.*

> *Praised be You, my Lord, through Sister Mother Earth,
> who sustains us and governs us and who produces
> varied fruits with colored flowers and herbs....*
>
> *In fact, the world beyond is so intimately entwined in
> our own natures that unconsciously we identify our more
> vivid perspectives of it with ourselves... The body is part of
> the external world, continuous with it. In fact, it is just
> as much a part of nature as anything else there – a river,
> a mountain, or a cloud. If we are fussily exact, we cannot
> define where our body begins and external nature ends...
> there is no definite boundary to determine where the body
> begins and external nature ends.[7]*

We need an ecological spirituality that gives birth to an ecological civilization.[8] Healthy theology proclaims a life-supporting vision of reality in which all creatures praise God and deserve our reverence. Healthy theological reflection leads to holy simplicity that inspires us personally and institutionally to live simply so that others may simply live, motivated by biophilia, love of the Earth-inspired by an Earth-loving God. Alfred North Whitehead asserts that "ideas won't keep. Something must be done about them."[9] Today, what won't keep is a creative and sustainable response to global climate change and a commitment to the well-being of the human and non-human worlds for decades to come. We can't wait for others; we must be the change we seek in the world. This idea won't keep: we need a theology and spirituality that inspires prayer and protest to save the planet.

One of the most important theological documents of the twenty-first century is Pope Francis' *Laudato Si*. In addressing the

---

7   Alfred North Whitehead, *Modes of Thought* (New York: Free Press, 1968), 21, 161.

8   Philip Clayton and William Andrew Schwartz, *What is Ecological Civilization: Crisis, Hope, and the Future of the Planet* (Anoka, WI: Process Century Press, 2019).

9   Lucien Price, *Dialogues with Alfred North Whitehead* (New York: Free Press, 1968), 116.

climate crisis which threatens the survival of humankind and the non-human world, Pope Francis abandoned the safe harbors of traditionalism to embrace the high hopes of a spiritual adventure in which humans can choose to become God's companions in healing the Earth.

Pope Francis titles his encyclical *Laudato Si* after Francis of Assisi's "Canticle of Creation" and begins his ecological treatise by paying homage to the one he describes as the patron saint of ecology.

> *"LAUDATO SI', mi' Signore"* – *"Praise be to you, my Lord"*. In the words of this beautiful canticle, Saint Francis of Assisi reminds us that our common home is like a sister with whom we share our life and a beautiful mother who opens her arms to embrace us. "Praise be to you, my Lord, through our Sister, Mother Earth, who sustains and governs us, and who produces various fruit with coloured flowers and herbs"[10]

Pope Francis condemns our materialism, greed, and alienation of nature and sees the way of Francis as a model for responding to climate change. The Gospel of Creation, Pope Francis affirms, is grounded in the goodness of creation, the holiness of human and non-human life, and the essential interdependence of planetary healing and institutional justice. Again, Pope Francis lauds Francis of Assisi's vision of a living earth in which every creature deserves our ethical consideration and reverence.

> [Francis] was particularly concerned for God's creation and for the poor and outcast. He loved, and was deeply loved for his joy, his generous self-giving, his openheartedness. He was a mystic and a pilgrim who lived in simplicity and in wonderful harmony with God, with others, with nature and with himself. He shows us just how inseparable the bond is

---

10   Pope Francis, ENCYCLICAL LETTER *LAUDATO SI* OF THE HOLY FATHER FRANCIS ON CARE FOR OUR COMMON HOME, section 1 (Laudato si' (24 May 2015) | Francis (vatican.va).

between concern for nature, justice for the poor, commitment to society, and interior peace.[11]

Inspired by Francis's vision, Pope Francis challenges us to recognize that "the urgent challenge to protect our common home includes a concern to bring the whole human family together to seek a sustainable and integral development, for we know that things can change."[12]

In the following sections, I will elaborate on ways Franciscan and Whiteheadian theology and spirituality can inspire a life-transforming ecological consciousness, embracing human and non-human life in the quest for justice and healing.

FRANCIS' LIVING UNIVERSE

Whitehead asserts that the world lives by the incarnation of God, whose aim is the production of Beauty from souls to cells and geodes to galaxies. Greatness in the life of a civilization and a person is characterized by its commitment to joining God in the production, preservation, and affirmation of beauty. As the Second Christ, a truly civilized and fully human being, Francis of Assisi was the incarnation of universal Beauty who saw God's incarnate love animating all creation. He experienced Beauty and Amazement in encountering the non-human world as well as the human face. Francis' relationship to the non-human world was his witness to width and depth of God's creativity and love. In the spirit of Francis, Bonaventure and Whitehead, along with Pope Francis, give us a theological vision for reverencing and affirming life in all its diversity. Clare reminds us to see Christ in the suffering of creation and imitate God's love for the least of these in the non-human and human world. Clare's vision reminds us that Christ is crucified on Calvary and also in the death of coral reefs, starvation as the result of climate influenced famine, and violence against immigrants and marginalized people.

---

11   Ibid., section 10.
12   Ibid., section 13.

Francis of Assisi lives in a God-filled enchanted universe, a world in which the heavens declare the glory of God, rocks cry out, sparrows prayed, and wolves can experience spiritual transformation. The first Franciscan biographer Thomas of Celano describes Francis' vision of life in terms of the unity of humankind and the non-human world characterized by reverence not exploitation and empathy not destruction.

> Fields and vineyards,
> Rocks and woods,
> all the beauties of the field,
> flowing springs and gardens,
> earth and fire, air and wind;
> all these he urged to love of God and to willing service.
> Finally, he used to call all creatures
> by the name of "brother" and "sister"
> and in a wonderful way, unknown to others,
> he could discern the secrets of the heart of creatures
> like someone who had already passed
> into the freedom of the glory of the children of God.[13]

As I have noted throughout this book, Francis affirmed that humankind belongs to a world of praise in which each creature's experience reflects the wisdom and creativity of God. When the Gospel of John says, "for God so loved the world," that means the "cosmos" in its in entirety not just wayward humanity. (John 3:16) When Jesus speaks of the birds of the air and the lilies of the field as objects of God's providential care, he invites us to be God's companions in healing the earth and its creatures as well as learning from the non-human world.

For eight centuries, people have been inspired by stories of Francis' nature mysticism and his loving interaction with the non-human world. Francis loved the non-human world, and the non-human world reciprocated in love for him. Doves and crows delighted in the saint's presence, listening with rapt attention.

---

13 *Francis of Assisi – The Saint: Early Documents*, 251.

Francis regularly blessed his human and non-human companions with the sign of the cross as well as with spoken benedictions. Once, after preaching a sermon to the birds, Francis "accused himself of negligence because he had not preached to them before." From then on Francis "carefully exhorted all birds, all animals, all reptiles, and also insensible creatures, to praise and love the Creator, because daily, invoking the name of the Savior, he observed their obedience in his own experience."[14] On another occasion, as he was giving a sermon, Francis noticed that swallows were chirping with such great joy that his human audience could not hear his message, provoking Francis' admonition, "My sister swallows, now it is the time for me to speak, since you have already said enough. Listen to the word of the Lord and stay quiet and calm until the word of the Lord is completed." In response, the sparrows listened rapt attention rivaling that of his human audience.[15] Challenged by the scriptural confession, "I am a worm and not a man," Francis discerned the holiness of the worms he encountered in the course his pilgrimages. Like practitioners of the Jain way of wisdom, Francis sought to avoid injuring his non-human kin. Thomas of Celano notes that "that is why he used to pick them up from the road and put them in a safe place so that they would not be crushed by the footsteps of passersby."[16] Francis even took care to see the light of God in the sparks issuing from his campfire. Truly, as the panentheistic motto proclaims, Francis saw:

> God in all things
> And all things in God.

Our worship of God is reflected not only in the way we treat persons with leprosy but in our attitudes and behavior toward the non-human world. Will we see the non-human world as a reflection of divine love or material to manipulate? Surely, we love the Creator by loving God's creatures. Francis was cognizant that

---

14 Ibid., 235.
15 Ibid., 235.
16 Ibid., 250.

our care for the soil reflects our commitment to God and reverence for God's creation. According to Thomas of Celano, his first biographer:

> When he washed his hands, he chose a place where water would not be trampled underfoot by his washings. Whenever he had to walk over rocks, he would walk with fear and reverence out of love for him who is called "The Rock."
>
> He also told the brother who cut the wood for fire not to cut down the whole tree, but to cut it in such a way that one part remained while the other was cut…He used to tell the brother who took care of the garden not to cultivate all the ground in the garden for vegetables, but to leave a piece of the ground that would produce wild plants that in their season would produce "Brother Flowers." Moreover, he used to tell the brother gardener that he should make a beautiful flower bed in the same part of the garden, planting and cultivating every variety of fragrant plants and those producing beautiful flowers.[17]

While Francis may not have fully developed a theology of ecology, his life proclaimed God's love for all creation, the universality of experience and value, and our moral responsibility to the non-human world. Our calling is to companion and protect rather than destroy and manipulate the non-human world and to weigh the needs of our non-human kin in our institutional, governmental, and economic decisions. Long before the emergence of the animal rights movement, Francis recognized our obligations to be gardeners and healers, friends and companions, and not destroyers of our planet and its non-human residents. The pioneer of the green and ecological movements, I believe that if Francis was alive today, he would be on the boat with Greenpeace, sitting in protest with Greta Thunberg, writing strict creation-affirming environmental protection regulations and legislation, and

---

[17] Francis of Assisi, *Early Documents*, volume 2, edited by Regis J. Armstrong, Wayne Hellman, and William Short (New York: New City Press, 1999), 192,

applauding Pope Francis along with ensuring that every human had adequate housing, nutrition, education, health care, and legal rights.

Bonaventure lived long before human caused climate change and environmental destruction threatened humankind and the planet as a whole. Yet, Bonaventure took a different path than those who identified spirituality with escape from the embodied world and its challenges. Drawing toward God, according to world-denying mystics, required turning your back on the earth and its beauties in in the wondrous diversity of the world. In contrast, Bonaventure recognized that spiritual growth not only involved turning from the many to the One but also affirming the presence of the One in the many. World affirming spirituality involves honoring the beauties of the earth as reflections of God's fountain of light and love and inspiration to seek the Beauty that never fades. Franciscan theology is God centered and affirms that centering in God means loving God in the world of the flesh by treating the ambient world in responsible and reverential ways and seeing our bodies as a temple, reflecting divine wisdom. Bonaventure's comment on God's omnipresence bears repeating:

> [God is] within all things, but not enclosed;outside all
> things, but not excluded;
> above all things, but not aloof;
> below all things, but not debased.
> Finally, because it is supremely one and all-inclusive,
> it is therefore,
> all in all…
> from him, in him, and through him are all things.[18]

God is all in all and God's energy of love is present in and through all things. To say that that God is: "An infinite sphere (or circle)/Whose center is everywhere/and whose circumference is nowhere" is to embrace the vision of a God-saturated universe

---

18 Bonaventure, *The Journey into God, The Tree of Life, The Life of St. Francis*, 100-101.

in which every creature is centered in God and God's love embraces all creatures without exception. If we truly believe that God is omnipresent, or present everywhere and in all things, our calling is to honor and delight in creation even when we must plant, cultivate, reap, and kill for our own survival. In a God-filled universe, every meal is a eucharistic celebration in which we express our gratitude to the plants and animals who give us life and energy and vow to treat their kin on air, earth, land, and sea as holy. Such a vision of God's world has no place for slogans such as "drill, baby, drill," "whoever dies with the most toys wins," or "winning isn't everything, it's the only thing." God's world is a community of communities in which God's love for the world inspires us to love, nurture, and honor diversity in its many forms. Thomas of Celano described Francis as a living prayer, and our calling is walk with humility and prayerfulness in our economics, politics, professional lives, and relationships. Prayerful environmentalism and economics delight in the planet, rejoice in beauty, trim away materialistic clutter, simplify life, and uplift the vulnerable. Today's Franciscan spirit sees the Earth as our Mother and all creatures as our kin, who must be nurtured and protected, and who call us to simplicity of life and sacrificial living.

WHITEHEAD'S GOD-FILLED WORLD

Process theology is a theology of earth, sky, sea, and land. Over fifty years ago, I discovered John Cobb's, *Is It Too Late?* the first full-length Christian theology of ecology, penned in 1971. Process theologians have been leaders in environmental theology and the quest for a sustainable civilization. In this section, I briefly outline Whitehead's vision of a living and God-filled world as an inspiration to place environmental issues at the center of our spiritual and political lives.

Whitehead and process theologians inspired by his vision assert that our world view shapes our ethics, politics, and lifestyle. Our religious beliefs can lead to actions and public policies that may heal or destroy the planet. We can promote life or death in our theologically inspired attitude toward the Earth. Transactional understandings of salvation focus on believing doctrines that assert that Jesus is the only path to heaven and that the doctrine of the Second Coming of Jesus is immanent. Such doctrines turn our attention from this world to the next or encourage domination over the non-human world. With our gaze fixed on heaven, what happens here on earth truly doesn't matter for our salvation. Further, if God intends to destroy the earth as prelude to a new heaven and earth, this world is of secondary importance and concern with the environment can be discarded in favor of drilling and profiting till Jesus comes again. Moreover, if we speak of God in terms of omnipotence or predestination, then the future of the planet is already settled and there's nothing we can do about it except prepare for the last judgment and afterlife. Historically, the doctrine of an authoritarian God has empowered "his" most ardent sycophants to claim God's authority to dominate the planet, using it solely for our purposes rather than seeing the non-human world as our kin, beloved by God and deserving our ethical consideration. To those motivated by authoritarian visions of God, dominion has also led to subjugating indigenous peoples, dominating and civilizing them in accordance with the values and beliefs of our superior religion and civilization. God has given us a "manifest destiny" to dominate and destroy whatever stands in the way of colonization, profit-making, and progress. Whatever we "discover" is ours even if it is already occupied by indigenous peoples. Empowered by God's sovereign authority, we act on the belief that God is on our side and those who differ from us must be converted, dominated, or destroyed, just as we do the natural world around us.

In contrast to domineering and destructive visions of God, Whitehead visualizes a universe and planet characterized by interdependence, relationship, experience, and value grounded in God's omnipresence and relational vision. Whitehead affirms a God who truly cares for the world and whose experience is shaped by the joy and sadness, and beauty and ugliness, of the world.

What we do matters to God. Our lives are our gifts to God and one another. God feels the pain of the pangolin and the osprey as dearly as God feels the pain of a toddler in Gaza or an elder in the United States. Our aspiration is to universal piety and world loyalty and to follow the counsel of Abraham Lincoln, who prayed not the God be on our side but that we be on God's side in embodying God's movements in the moral and spiritual arcs of history.

Interdependence. The whole world conspires to create each moment of experience, notes Alfred North Whitehead. Moreover, in our dynamic and interdependent universe, everything is everywhere, all at once. A butterfly flaps their wings in Pacific Grove, California, leading eventually to raindrops at the Chautauqua Institution in New York where I am writing these words in August 2024. Increases in water temperature, the result of climate change, create factors contributing to longer and more severe hurricane seasons. A stepmother's personal care and interest in a boy's intellectual life inspires him to a thirst for knowledge and eventually the vocation of becoming America's greatest president, who even in time of war called USA citizens to follow the better angels of our nature. Humankind is embedded in the non-human world. "If we are fussily exact, we cannot define where our body begins and external nature ends…there is no definite boundary to determine where the body begins and external nature ends."[19] Whitehead would appreciate Carl Sagan's words descriptive of our personal and planetary lives.

> The cosmos is within us. We are made of star-stuff. We are a way for the universe to know itself. Some part of our being knows this is where we came from. We long to return. We can because the cosmos is within us.
>
> The beauty of a living thing is not the atoms that go into it, but the way those atoms are put together…We are all connected. To each other, biologically; to the Earth, chemically;

---

19 Alfred North Whitehead, *Modes of Thought* (New York: Free Press, 1968), 21, 161.

to the rest of the universe, anatomically. Our planet, our society, and we ourselves are a part of a vast, cosmic arena. We are, each of us, a little universe.

Joined intimately with the non-human natural world around us, we are inspired to show gratitude for the gifts of Mother Earth with head, hands, and heart. In gratitude for our Generous Mother, herself a planetary reflection of Divine Wisdom, we touch the earth lightly, caring for the foundations of life and seeing the world around us as the Temple of God in whom we live and move and have our being. (Acts 17:28) With Folliott Sandford Pierpoint, lyricist of the hymn, "For the Beauty of the Earth," we join in praise that turns us toward action to heal the earth.

> For the beauty of the earth,
> For the glory of the skies,
> For the love which from our birth
> Over and around us lies—
> Lord of all, to Thee we raise,
> This our hymn of grateful praise.
> For the wonder of each hour,
> Of the day and of the night,
> Hill and vale, and tree and flow'r,
> Sun and moon, and stars of light—
> Lord of all, to Thee we raise,
> This our hymn of grateful praise.[20]

Joined with all life, we recognize that we are a part of Nature, not apart from nature. What we do in economics and public policy can cure or kill, ensure survival or put planetary life in jeopardy. If we neglect our interdependence, treating Nature as unfeeling matter totally at our disposal, our actions will contribute to extreme weather, forest fires, devastating hurricanes, drought and flood, and the consequent reality of climate immigration. In contrast, recognizing our interdependence, balancing self-interest and world loyalty are seen to be two aspects of responsible stew-

---

[20] Folliott Sandford Pierpoint, "For the Beauty of the Earth." (1863)

ardship. We care for the earth to ensure the flourishing of future generations and in so doing promote well-being in the non-human world.

Experience and Value. Pan-experientialism, or panpsychism, is at the heart of Whitehead's world view. Reality is constituted of interdependent drops of experience. Experience characterizes quanta particles and the ecstasy of mystics. Cells and souls alike feel their world. Recognizing the ubiquity and various levels of experience, we discover that we are not lost in the cosmos. We are part of an experiential value creating world. Wherever we find ourselves, we are on holy ground. As Jacob stammers after dreaming of a ladder of angels ascending from Earth to Heaven and back to Earth, "God is in this place, and I did not know it." Experience is everywhere, and so is value, and the recognition of value gives birth to reverence for life. We cannot intentionally deface the value experience at the heart of reality, Whitehead mandates. Although "life is robbery," that is, all life destroys or ingests to survive, we must be judicious in our harm of experiencing, valuing beings. All things deserve our moral consideration. Our affirmation of the uniqueness of human existence must occur in the context of affirming the value of non-human existence. Recognizing the universality of value, embodied in Francis' world of praise and Whitehead's living universe, challenges us to minimize harm and maximize nurture and protection of the non-human world.

The interdependent, relational, and all-loving God. For Whitehead, God is the primary example and, in my interpretation, everlasting ground of the dynamic and interdependent nature of things. God and the world are in constant relationship. While the divine fountain of love may be ontologically prior, as the source of the energy and aim of each creature, God and the world constantly shape one another. God is in all things and all things are in God in the creative process of every possible universe and in the concreteness of our interdependent dynamic universe and planetary community. As creative-responsive love, God not only provides each creature the vision for what it can become, God also experiences the world, part and whole. God makes a difference to every creature and every creature makes a difference to God. In terms of the ecology of life, our actions matter to God. God feels the pain of dying species, the anxiety of young persons fearing what global climate change may mean for their future, and the hopelessness of climate refugees. What we do touches God just as what God does touches us. We have the opportunity in our relationships to give God a more beautiful or uglier world. If we fail in our response to climate change, God will feel the pain of countless dying humans and non-humans. The question to us is clear, with earth in the balance, our calling is to do something beautiful for God by loving the human and non-human world.

As the Heart of the Universe, God treasures all things. All things not only valuable in themselves; they are also valuable because God loves and inspires them. There is something of God in each creature. As such, to deface the non-human and human worlds is to dishonor God, not a punitive God or rule making God, but a God who feels the pain of our destruction of the non-human world and one another. God loves the world and wants us to love it as well. In a truly God-filled world, as I noted earlier, we honor every being, minimizing the harm we do to the non-human world, and giving thanks for the non-human realm as we recognize the necessary destruction of non-human life needed for our survival and flourishing.

God loves a world in which creatures are at cross purposes and humans have differing and often contrasting and conflicting needs. Still, God continues to love and evoke the quest for beauty in spite of the realities of creaturely caused pain and suffering. Recognizing our solidarity with suffering creation and its Creator, we make a commitment to love God by loving God's world, and in our love for the world, we join God in the quest to heal the Earth.

SPIRITUAL PRACTICES FOR GLOBAL HEALERS

Healing the planet is the gift of spiritual connection. We are one with earth, sea, sky, and land. The pangolin, Right Whale, firefly, and sparrow are our kin. They speak to us, and we can share our lives with them. God loves the whole earth, and proclaims it good, and invites us to delight in the beauty of the earth and from that delight become gardeners and healers of the world in companionship with God and our non-human kin.

Holy Poverty. Although few of us will take vows of poverty, we can embrace holy simplicity and spiritual decluttering.[1] We can, in words traditionally attributed to Saint Elizabeth Ann Seton, who counseled "live simply so others may simply live." Take time to examine your lifestyle as you consider the Franciscan and Whiteheadian call to be a global citizen and advocate for ecojustice. Consider:

- Where can you simplify your life as it relates to time commitments, complexity, and possessions?
- Where do you see yourself cluttering your life with activities and material objects?
- What do you truly need to experience peace and well-being?
- Where should you be more generous in your care for others and the earth?
- What practices and policies should you advocate in the political realm?
- What truly brings you joy? What might bring joy and well-being to vulnerable persons and the marginalized in your community and the planet?

Advocate for Ecojustice. While neither Francis nor Whitehead were political activists, their theological and spiritual vision in-

---

[1] Bruce Epperly, *Spiritual Decluttering* (Gonzalez, FL: Energion Publications, 2019).

spires the interplay of environmental healing and justice seeking. We are global citizens as well as citizens of our nation, who need to become informed about the relationship of environmental destruction with poverty, immigration, disease, sexism, and racism. In an interdependent world, everything is connected, and our actions can contribute to healing or destruction, and life or death, for millions. In the wake of your research, consider ways you can become politically involved, "acting locally and thinking globally." You can surround your actions with prayer and peaceful reconciliation even with those who sacrifice the planet for personal power or gain. They too are God's children and our kin. You may choose to prayerfully to:

- Contribute and become active in an environmental justice group, such as Third Act (Bill McKibben's group for retired citizens), Greenpeace, Environmental Defense Fund.
- Contact your political leaders advocating on behalf of greater environmental legislation and regulation. Learn about and become involved in environmental issues in your local community.
- Challenge all forms of sexism, racism, poverty, and ecological injustice and support candidates for whom the healing of persons and the planet is a priority.
- Organize, in the spirit of Francis, a group that joins contemplation and environmental action, and connects simplicity of life with our relationship with God.

Holy Sensing. Franciscan and Whiteheadian spirituality are highly sensate. The Holy speaks to us in each occasion of experience, and in the heavens above and the ambient environment. All creation is kin. The fountain of light, love, and divine creativity flows in and through us and with us in the world around us. In this practice, simply "open your senses" to the World of Praise, feeling the breeze, hearing the singing birds, bathing in sunlight, delighting in the face of a child, savoring your meals, giving thanks for all creatures great and small. Let yourself be filled with awe and wonder at the beauty of our Good Earth and its creatures, yourself included.

Awaken each morning in gratitude for God's wondrous world of beauty, energy, love, and praise, and choose to be a love-finder and beauty-creator in each action throughout the day. Say "yes" to life in its abundance. Become an ambassador for Beauty. Praise God!

Apostles of Ecological Civilization. Humankind cannot avoid having an impact on the non-human world. Every creature changes its environment. Survival, not to mention flourishing and evolving, requires non-humans as well as humans to be part of a process of "altering their environment in favor of the immediate desires of their species."[2] Accordingly, "to achieve ecological civilization would not be to give up modifying nature, but to learn to do so in ways that we can learn from nature and from its success in creating ecosystems that over time increase in complexity and richness."[3] We need to get beyond "us" versus "them" in our relationships with other nations, our human kin, and the non-human world as we seek "a holistic vision of all aspects of society…in terms of the ecological frame."[4] We need to see learning, praying, and acting as different aspects of one another. To study is to pray and this means learning about ecosystems and ways we can live in harmony, healing and not destroying. Praying means committing ourselves to advocacy and protest, and joining faith, economics, and citizenship in quest of a sustainable and healthy world. In an interdependent world, everything we do can make a difference. We can do small things, such as using less energy, recycling, and minimizing our use of non-renewable products. We can also be part of larger circles of planetary healing through advocacy and

---

2 John Cobb, "What is Ecological Civilization," in *What is Ecological Civilization,* 1.
3 Ibid., 2.
4 Ibid., 10.

volunteerism. We can prayerfully become part of larger organizations whose goals involve changes in economics and public policy to heal the earth.

6
INSTRUMENTS OF PEACE

WHERE ALL ARE PILGRIMS AND NONE ARE STRANGERS

> *In all his preaching, before he presented the word of God to the assembly, he prayed for peace, saying, "May the Lord give you peace."*[5]
>
> *Peace is the removal of inhibition and not its destruction. It results in a wider sweep of conscious interest. It enlarges the field of attention. Thus peace is self-control at its widest, — at the width in where the "self" has been lost, and interest has been transferred to coordinations wider than personality …[The fruit of peace] is the love of mankind as such…Peace is the understanding of tragedy, and at the same time its preservation.*[6]

Following Francis of Assisi, "Grant us your peace" is my daily prayer for my grandchildren, friends and family, nation, and planet. It is my prayer for myself as I seek to balance personal relationships and citizenship with my personal needs. I begin

---

5   *Francis of Assisi: The Saint – Early Documents*, 200.
6   Alfred North Whitehead, *Adventures in Ideas*, 285-286.

my predawn walk each morning with the prayer, "Lord, make me an instrument of your peace."

The elusive quest for peace is at the heart of the spiritual pilgrimage. Yet, authentic peace must join our inner life with the outside world and our responsibility to be peacemakers in an increasingly precarious time, in which the realities of war, racism, political violence, incivility, and climate change confront us the moment we turn on the news or log onto to the internet. The information technologies and social media intended to bring us closer to each other have tragically accelerated our divisions, siloing us from kin in our respective alternative realities, and exacerbating our differences to the point that the soul of the nation and the spirit of the planet are disintegrating. In affirmation of social media, and platforms such as Zoom, study groups bring people together from across the globe: people from around the country attend my weekly Zoom Bible Study and I regularly do cameo lectures for groups using my books or interested in the interplay of theology and spirituality. Still, the quest to join common ground along with higher ground seems futile as the soul of the nation plunges into chaos and authoritarian powers, many of which find their inspiration in nationalist and orthodox faith traditions that threaten to destroy democracy and eliminate diversity. Yet, beyond conflict and competition, deep down, our quest is for peace. Even the most divisive and self-centered of us are in search of the experience of calm and contentment which comes about when inner and outer peace are joined and each person has the opportunity to fulfill the deepest, divinely inspired, desires of their hearts.

Francis, Clare, Bonaventure, and Whitehead placed peace at the center of their visions of the human adventure. Francis, his spiritual companions, and Whitehead lived in times of international conflict, the Crusades and two world wars. They knew that the path to inner peace could only occur when people transferred their focus from self-interest to world loyalty and from individualism to community. While both Whitehead and Francis treasured solitude, and saw prayerful contemplation as essential to spiritual growth, they realized that personal well-being and social justice are interconnected and that peace on earth and peace in the human heart emerge from a vision of interdependence and global unity. Whiteheadian and Franciscan spirituality embodies the Southern African affirmation, *ubuntu*, "I am because of you. We are because of one another."

FRANCIS' WAY OF PEACE

Francis is the theologian of peace. While Francis did not write a treatise on peacemaking, his life – like the life of Jesus – is the embodiment of God's vision of Shalom, which earned him Bonaventure's affirmation as the "Second Christ." It is up to us in the twenty-first century to provide a theology of peace and healing to give voice to the way of Jesus and Francis. Francis' vision of peace incarnates Jesus' Sermon on the Mount in its embrace of otherness, care for the infirm and vulnerable, reconciliation with our nation's enemies, and empathy with the non-human world as God's Beloved children, worthy of our love and capable of becoming our companions as God's healers of the earth.

"Let your life speak," proclaims Quaker spirituality and Francis' life shouted peace wherever he went and with whomever he encountered. More than a garden statue, Francis and his spiritual companions give us guidance for our relationships, professional lives, and political involvement. Listen to Bonaventure's description of the Little Poor One's voice of peace:

> At the beginning and ending of every sermon [Francis] announced peace; in every greeting he wished for peace; in every contemplation he sighed for ecstatic peace-like the citizen of that city of Jerusalem of whichthat Man of Peace says; who was peaceable with those who hated peace. Pray for the peace of Jerusalem.[7]

---

7   Bonaventure, *The Soul's Journey into God, The Tree of Life, The Life of St. Francis,* 53-54.

Francis' and his followers embodied Jesus' path of peace in a world characterized by violence and division based on politics, class, and economics. In thirteenth century Italy, there was little common ground between rich and poor, priests and laypeople, Christians and Muslims, healthy and sick, and one town and another. Persons with leprosy were viewed pariahs and unclean outcasts, as they were in Jesus' time. Like most of his contemporaries, Francis was deathly afraid of persons with leprosy. While Francis gave persons with leprosy alms, he avoided close contact until God transformed his heart, showing him that persons with leprosy were God's beloved children, deserving of our reverence and love. No longer afraid of these "others," in a pivotal moment of spiritual transformation, Francis embraced a man with leprosy, and from then on could be found directly ministering to leper communities. Francis discovered that in Christ, there was neither healthy nor sick, insider or outsider. Regardless of our social status or health condition, we are all connected and joined in God's world of praise.

During the era of the Crusades (1095-1291), Christians and Muslims saw each other as infidels unworthy of compassion or ethical consideration. Both sides believed that killing their religious enemy or dying in battle guaranteed eternal life. Popes promised nobles and their wealthy subjects that financing crusades to retake the Holy Land would be rewarded by the remission of sins and release from the pain of purgatorial cleansing. In this time of religious violence and hatred, Francis crossed boundaries, risking his life and reputation to engage in spiritual dialogue with Sultan Malik al-Kamil in Damietta, Egypt. Francis and the Sultan spoke respectfully to one another as God's beloved children. While the Sultan was not persuaded to follow the faith of Jesus or Francis to follow Mohammed, Francis' biographer reports that "the Sultan was overflowing with admiration and recognized him as a man unlike any other. He was moved by his words and listened to him very willingly."[8]

Francis transcended "otherness" in approaching the Muslim political leader, viewed by many of Francis' fellow Christians as

---

8   *Francis and Clare: The Early Documents – The Saint*, 231.

an enemy of the one true faith and worthy of death as an idolator and infidel. In this relationship with the Muslim ruler, Francis models a path to creative interfaith relationships and relationships with doubters, seekers, agnostics, and atheists, and in our time, people of differing political perspectives. In the spirit of what Ilia Delio describes of the "humility of God" who receives as well as gives in relationship to the world, Francis shares his faith and also listens to the Sultan share his faith. In their conversation, Francis reveals that Christians can learn and grow from relationships with persons of other religious traditions. Even if we remain unconvinced of their ultimate truth, we can treat persons of other faiths, theological perspectives, and political viewpoints with respect and reverence and strive to learn from our encounters. We can honor the divine in persons of other faith traditions, trusting that God is at work in their lives as well as our own.

Francis' vision of a democracy of spirit, described in the "Canticle of the Creatures," inspires us to look for truth and beauty everywhere. All God's creatures reveal something of their Creator and can be vehicles of revelation to us. Wherever truth and healing are found, God is its source, whether in other religious traditions, science laboratories, or critiques from religious "outsiders." Beneath enmity, there is divinity. In a world of division and exclusion, belief in the faithfulness to the God whose circumference embraces the "other" inspired a cosmopolitan open spirited faith. The "others" are also God's children and our love for them reflects God's love for us and all creation. Francis reminds us that we are one in God's Spirit. There is no other, alien to us and outside of the circle of divine love and inspiration.

In Francis' world, class and economics determined virtually everything about a person's daily life and relationships. The poor were mandated to respect their "betters," whether they were priests, nobles, or the rising upper class like Francis', Clare's, and Bonaventure's family. In a world where riding on horseback was a sign of status, Francis walked as a sign of solidarity in contrast to the regal carriages of the pope and bishops, and their entourages.

Francis was a person of the people, who saw himself as one with the poor, infirm, diseased, as well as the non-human world. God is as fully present in the peasant farmer and shopkeeper as the prince and pope.

One of the best-known stories of Francis' life involves his healing relationship with a dangerous wolf and the frightened people of the Umbrian village of Gubbio. Terrorized by what they perceived as a vicious predator, the people of Gubbio seldom entered the forest except to hunt for their lupine enemy. As the lover of all creation, who experienced holiness in sparrows, worms, and rabbits, Francis sought out the wolf to resolve this deadly conflict. When the wolf saw Francis, the vicious predator initially charged at him, ready to pounce on his perceived enemy, but stopped in his tracks when Francis made the sign of the cross. Then the humble preacher admonished the wolf for his violent behavior and invited the wolf to claim God's path of peace, demanding that it refrain from attacking the townspeople and their domestic animals. Francis saw something of God in the fierce predator as he looked into the wolf's eyes and the wolf heard God's voice as Francis spoke to him. Deep down, the wolf realized that he had a higher destiny than killing and terrorizing. When Francis returned to the village, he gave the wary villages a similar command: welcome the wolf as a fellow citizen, provide the wolf with a home, and ensure that he was fed and cared for. The once vicious wolf and the once frightened villagers experienced a conversion of heart, recognizing their common identity as God's creatures and learning to live in peace.

As we read the stories of Francis, we are challenged to ask ourselves" "Can politics be peaceful? Can we be both prophets and healers, social activists and agents of reconciliation? Can we advocate with passion for Earth care, justice, and equality without succumbing to divisiveness and incivility?" This is an important question since historically, and now more than ever with incivility, dishonesty, and hatred regularly weaponized in social media, the contour of our political rhetoric and policy is often win-lose, binary, divisive, and hate-filled. Gone are the days of the "loyal opposition," in which USA Americans assumed the good faith of those who politically differ from us and whose mutual respect inspired common ground on issues of national concern. We need a new vision that awakens us to politics and citizenship as sacred vocations intended to bring wholeness and well-being to our communities.

The key for a Franciscan vision of social and political transformation is to be found in Francis' "Canticle of the Creatures," which affirms the sacredness of all life forms and sees humanity in its wondrous variety as intimately connected with its non-human companions. Whatever or whomever praises God, and for Francis that is all creation, human and non-human, deserves our ethical consideration and transcends any differences between us experientially, geographically, and politically. You can be as persistent as Francis was in seeking papal approval for his emerging order and assertive as Clare in her quest to draft the Rule of the Poor Sisters, rather than accepting a patriarchal and ecclesiastical document, while remaining civil and seeing the holiness of those who stand in the way of your ideals. Every encounter can be an opportunity for partnership and healing. Honest and heart-felt diversity reflects God's diverse presence in the world and is a call to spiritual transformation and self-transcendence.

As a monastic professor and administrator as well as priest, Bonaventure spent much of his professional life as Minister General of the Franciscan Order. When a schism arose between the itinerant monks imitating the houseless life of Francis and those, like himself, who were housed in universities and monasteries, Bonaventure led a process of reconciliation which honored both the itinerant origins of the Order and the role of an educated and stable monastic life in the preservation of Francis' vision. Diversity in lifestyle and practice need not to be the source of division but can add intensity, creativity, and beauty to a community's life. In his final years, Bonaventure was asked to be a leader in the reconciliation of the Western and Eastern churches. In the spirit of his mentor Francis of Assisi, Bonaventure possessed the spiritual and intellectual bandwidth to see beyond his own perspective to honor and learn from the unique spirituality of the Eastern church. As a proto-ecumenist, Bonaventure sought a "creative synthesis," to use Whiteheadian language, which honored the gifts of both traditions, realized that complexity and variety enrich a community, and invited communities to move forward inspired by new possibilities rather than backward looking traditionalism.

If we see the divine in wolves, persons with leprosy, religious leaders whose views differ from our own, and political leaders of lands with which you are at war, then we can honor our gifts, treasure our viewpoints, and respect the perspectives of those who differ from us. We can put peace ahead of victory that humiliates our opponents and reconciliation above retribution that destroys any chance of global and personal healing.

In the Franciscan world, there is no "other." Everyone is centered and encircled by God's love and kin to us. Even our enemies and those who initially repulse us by their behavior or physical condition and appearance are God's beloved children, capable of praise and thanksgiving. A world of praise inspires us to look for common ground, heal divisions, and work for that "more perfect union" in which:

> The wolf shall live with the lamb;
>   the leopard shall lie down with the kid;
> the calf and the lion will feed together,
>   and a little child shall lead them.
> The cow and the bear shall graze;
>   their young shall lie down together;
> and the lion shall eat straw like the ox.
> The nursing child shall play over the hole of the asp,
>   and the weaned child shall put its hand on the adder's den.
> They will not hurt or destroy
>   on all my holy mountain,
> for the earth will be full of the knowledge of the LORD
>   as the waters cover the sea…(Isaiah 11:6-9)

In Francis' God-filled world of praise, "they shall beat their swords into plowshares and their spears into pruning hooks; nation shall not lift up sword against nation; neither shall they learn war anymore." (Isaiah 2:4) In companionship with another walking mystic Vietnamese Buddhist spiritual guide Thich Nhat Hanh, Francis proclaimed that "peace is every step" and that each moment is an opportunity for healing and reconciliation.

WHITEHEAD: PEACE AS SELF-TRANSCENDENCE

If Francis is the theologian of peace, then Alfred North Whitehead is the philosopher of peace in addition to being the metaphysician of divine love. Whitehead concludes his magisterial interpretation of Western civilization, *Adventures of Ideas,* with a chapter on peace, the personal and civic virtue that along with truth, adventure, and beauty, crowns civilized existence. Whitehead's Infinite and intimate God inspires an infinite and intimate vision of peace. To recapitulate the words with which this chapter began:

> Thus peace is self-control at its widest, - at the width in where the "self" has been lost, and interest has been transferred to coordinations wider than personality…[the fruit of peace] the love of mankind as such…Peace is the understanding of tragedy, and at the same time its preservation.[9]

Whether we look at individuals or institutions, peace involves what my teacher process theologian John B. Cobb describes as self-transcending selfhood. While much of the Western world exalts the individual, isolated self, Whitehead's ideal of selfhood is global and sacrificial in the healthiest sense of the world. Contrary to the image of rugged individualism reflected in the intransigent independence of the self-made person who holds on to my property, my rights, my guns, my money, and my nation, the person of peace finds "perfection," equanimity, and calm, in empathy rath-

---

9   Alfred North Whitehead, *Adventures of Ideas*, 285-286.

er than apathy, relationship rather than isolation, sacrifice rather than aggrandizement, and world loyalty rather than self-interest.

In their reflections on Holy Poverty, Francis and Clare assert the individualist always has something to lose and is always motivated by the desire to hold onto what they possess whether privilege, power, property, position, or even the possession of religious orthodoxy. The cosmopolitan person, and "cosmopolitan" means politically cosmic, the person whose soul seeks to be one with all creation in its cosmic perspective, places care for others as essential to one's own well-being. In the language of Jesus, the person of peace loves their neighbor as themselves and recognizes that God cares for the righteous and unrighteous alike. When others are enriched in healthy and just ways, we are enriched. When others are treated unjustly, we feel their pain. While remaining spiritually centered, the boundaries of our self-hood expand to embrace the well-being of others in all their diversity.

No one has described this large-souled sense of life's unity and interdependence than Martin Luther King, whose theological perspective was influenced by process theologian Henry Nelson Weiman.

> It all boils down to this, that all life is interrelated. We are caught in an inescapable network of mutuality, tied into a single garment of destiny. Whatever affects one directly affects all indirectly. We are made to live together because of the interrelated structure of reality.[10]

> For some strange reason I cannot be what I ought to be until you are what you ought to be. And you can never be what you ought to be until I am what I ought to be. That's the way the God's universe is made."[11]

---

10   Martin Luther King, Jr. *Testament of Hope: The Essential Writings and Speeches of Martin Luther King, Jr.* (edited by James M. Washington), (New York: HarperSanFrancisco, 1986), 254.
11   Martin Luther King, Jr., *A Knock at Midnight* (New York: Warner Books), 208.

The relational, persuasive, all-embracing, and empathetic God inspires a spirituality of empathy and hospitality. The universal God inspires universal compassion. Their vision of God's creative-responsive love takes persons of peace beyond punitive, fear-based, and binary relationships and politics, grounded in individualistic visions of God, to universalistic images of God and humankind. Love, not fear, and commitment to embodying the power of love and not the love of power, reflects a peaceful person's vision of God's empathetic presence in the world. We become, Whitehead asserts, like the God whom we envisage and follow.

> The new, and almost profane, concept of the goodness of God replaces the older emphasis on the will of God. In communal religion you study the will of God in order that he may preserve you. In a purified religion…you study his goodness in order to be like him. It is the difference between the enemy you conciliate and the companion whom you imitate.[12]

For some, to be like God is to divide the world into friend and foe, saved and unsaved, valuable and expendable. Their God institutionalizes otherness whether it involves politics, race, or salvation. Their God is spiritually brittle, vindictive, and unable to abide with diversity. For the God of Whitehead and the parents of Franciscan spirituality, the imitation of God leads to a very different ethic and politics: to experiences of unity, hospitality, compassion, and affirmation. God has stature and God's love embraces all creation. If God's fountain of love and night flows through, enlivening, energizing, and empowering all things, then we must let our love flow without boundaries or limitations. Two thousand years earlier, Jesus described God's all-inclusive love as the inspiration for our own spiritual stature.

> You have heard that it was said, "You shall love your neighbor and hate your enemy." But I say to you: Love your enemies and pray for those who persecute you, so that you may be children of your Father in heaven, for he makes his

---

12 Whitehead, *Religion in the Making*, 40.

sun rise on the evil and on the good and sends rain on the righteous and on the unrighteous. For if you love those who love you, what reward do you have? Do not even the tax collectors do the same? And if you greet only your brothers and sisters, what more are you doing than others? Do not even the gentiles do the same? Be perfect, therefore, as your heavenly Father is perfect. (Matthew 5:43-48)

Process theologian Bernard Loomer (1912-1985), one of my Claremont Graduate School professors, describes divine and human stature in terms of largeness of spirit. Too many of our "gods" are small spirited and easily offended and encourage small spirited religions who focus on retribution rather than healing. These gods and their followers appear strong, but beneath their threats and rhetoric, they live by fear and violence and begrudge any human achievement or success for persons other than themselves. They even hoard salvation, assuming if someone else, especially someone from another faith is saved, their salvation is in jeopardy. The God of peace and healing embraces all creation with love, honoring diversity and encouraging creativity and agency and serving as the model for our fullest humanity.

> By S-I-Z-E I mean the stature of a person's soul, the range and depth of his love, his capacity for relationships. I mean the volume of life you can take into your being and still maintain your integrity and individuality, the intensity and variety of outlook you can entertain in the unity of your being without feeling defensive or insecure. I mean the strength of your spirit to encourage others to become freer in the development of their diversity and uniqueness. I mean the power to sustain more complex and enriching tensions. I mean the magnanimity of concern to provide conditions that enable others to increase in stature.[13]

---

13 Loomer, Bernard M., "S-I-Z-E. is the Measure," Religious Experience and Process Theology, ed. Harry James Cargas and Bernard Lee (New York: Paulist Press, 1976), pp. 69-76

Like young Jesus at the Temple, who "grew in wisdom and stature," we can choose to be great souled persons, little Christs, mahatmas, and Bodhisattvas, who have no enemies and whose love is all embracing even in the conflictual world of politics. We can see diversity and division as a call to reconciliation and healing. Whitehead counsels a politics of beauty, in which we seek a "harmony of harmonies," or "community of communities," as citizens and political decision-makers. While we are citizens of the United States, we are also citizens of the world. While we seek to protect and nurture our families, the quest for peace mandates that we seek health and well-being for every family from every nation. While we honor our nation's just laws and support orderly border policing, the quest for peace requires us to recognize that immigrants are not threats but beloved children of God. We can behold the face of God the xenophobic white nationalist and MAGA hatted fear monger and also in the immigrant (Jesús, María y José) coming north from Central America or fleeing to Egypt. The world lives by the incarnation of God and God is incarnate in immigrants, struggling farmers, union picketers, persons of other faiths, and environmentalists and oil company executives.

We can seek a higher standard of living for every human across the globe and especially in overseas companies that produce products we purchase and also work for ecojustice that includes the non-human world. The adventurous and sustainable civilization we seek must of necessity utilize power and order to secure the well-being of future generations but must aim at employing as little coercion and harm as possible in the balance of rights and responsibilities. The power of compassionate persuasion and not domineering legality should be our goal. Practicing peace moves the moral and spiritual arcs of history toward the ever-evolving horizon of Beloved Community in which joyful companionship abounds and the sounds of the city streets and country byways are filled with the sounds of children's laughter.

SPIRITUAL PRACTICES FOR GLOBAL HEALERS

Peace is the heart of Franciscan and Whiteheadian spirituality. Peace is the gift of self-transcendence, empathy, and compassion. Peace emerges when we love our neighbor as ourselves and connect our own well-being with the well-being of neighbors and strangers.

Living the Spirit of Franciscan and Whiteheadian Peace. The quest for peace has been the underlying theme of this text. As I noted earlier in this text, every morning when I set out on my predawn walk, I say to myself, "God, make me an instrument of peace." I am seeking to embody the spirit of Jesus and Francis as inspiration for every encounter I will have in the day ahead. I recall Francis' practice of saying "Peace be with you" as he began each sermon and as greeted people in his pilgrim journey. In our time of incivility and divisiveness, we need to be agents of peace.

We can see peace and be the embodiment of peace in every situation. We can picket and pray. We can challenge and care. We can be firm in the quest for justice and also have peace as our goal. For Francis, in the spirit of Jesus, peace involved the intention to see Christ and be Christ to everyone he met. Centuries later the social activist mystic Dorothy Day stated that "I speak to persons as if they are angels."

Peace is the gift of self-transcendence in which our well-being is connected with the well-being of our neighbors. As we advance their lives, our own lives are enriched. Deep down, there is something of God in everyone. Deep down, even the most dysfunctional politician seeks wholeness and peace, and our quest for peace may be the catalyst for their experiencing their own holiness and the holiness of others. In our homes and in our citizenship, we need to remember the words of anti-war activist A.J. Muste, "There is no way to peace. Peace is the way." This has inspired me to pray for politicians whose policies and behavior I detest and to look beyond their cruel and vindictive exterior to see a child of God, mortal, frightened, and worried about the future like me.

Today on July 13, 2024, as I wrote these words, an assassination attempt was made on a USA presidential candidate, known for vitriolic and divisive speech. I was stunned by the event, and immediately recalled "The Prayer of Francis" to calm my spirit and awaken me to the better angels of my nature. This prayer, cited in chapter one, bears repeating for persons like me who are involved in challenging the injustices of our time. Initially, I did not intend to repeat the Prayer of St. Francis in this text, but the violence of the USA, and the anxiety of everyday life inspired me to include this prayer as an invitation to peace. We can calm our spirits so that peace comes with every breath. We can challenge the purveyors of violence and still them as God's beloved children. We can go beyond self-interest to self-transcendence and see everyone from a presidential candidate to the young persons who sought to assassinate him as God's beloved child. We can join peace in our hearts with peaceful advocacy for social transformation.

To embody the Franciscan and Whiteheadian visions of peace, I reiterate my invitation to you to read this prayer daily as a form of spiritual medication. As you begin the day, say "God, make me an instrument of peace" as you breathe deeply the Peace of Christ. Remember the prayer – simply the word "peace," accompanied by a deep breath and sense of unity, when you feel yourself becoming impatient, angry, and wishing to lash out at a companion, co-worker, family member, politician, or a customer service representative. Chant to yourself as you take a deep breath. "God make me an instrument of peace," and open your eyes to the holiness of the one whom you're tempted to insult or raise your voice. (I must confess that I keep this prayer handy and invoke it regularly to calm my spirit and inspire me to speak truth or share my impatience or frustration with kindness rather than vitriol and anger.) You can assert your rights and the rights of others, but let challenge come from a place of peace and healing.

Let us live by the spirit of this Franciscan prayer, repeating this, embracing the same spirit found in some of our companions who choose to repeat the Serenity Prayer hour by hour and day by day:

> Lord, make me an instrument of Your peace;
> Where there is hatred, let me sow love;
> Where there is injury, pardon;
> Where there is doubt, faith;
> Where there is despair, hope;
> Where there is darkness, light;
> And where there is sadness, joy.
> O Divine Master,
> Grant that I may not so much seek
> To be consoled as to console;
> To be understood, as to understand;
> To be loved, as to love;
> For it is in giving that we receive,
> It is in pardoning that we are pardoned,
> And it is in dying that we are born to Eternal Life.
> Amen.

Letting Your Self Grow. Whitehead defines peace as "self-control at its widest, - at the width in where the "self" has been lost, and interest has been transferred to co-ordinations wider than personality." When we lose or let go of our small self, letting it die, as Jesus says, a new and larger self is born. The isolated, anxious, competitive self gives way to a calm, cooperative, and supportive self. When we find ourselves, we become, as African American spiritual guide Howard Thurman says, friendly people living in a friendly world. We experience a world similar to that described by Thomas Merton in his recollection of a mystical experience that came to him in downtown Louisville:

> At the corner of Fourth and Walnut, in the center of the shopping district, I was suddenly overwhelmed with the realization that I loved all those people, that they were mine and I was theirs, that we could not be alien to one

another even though we were total strangers. It was like waking from a dream of separateness…The whole illusion of separate holy existence is a dream.[14]

In our unity, we discover that there is no "other," alien to us, despite the uniqueness of each person. In this practice, throughout the day repeat to yourself "there is no other." Whenever you are prone to ethically or relationally distance yourself from another, or to engage in judgment on those who differ, repeat "There is no other. We are one in God."

Throughout the day, look deeply at those around you. Honor their uniqueness. Feel a sense of unity with them, desiring that they receive the deepest, most authentic desires of their hearts. With the Buddhist sage, pray for the happiness and wholeness of all creatures and then work toward wholeness in every interaction, even those that involve challenge and critique.

As a citizen, follow a politics of stature, of large spiritedness. In the course of writing this text, I listened to an interview with William Barber on his latest book, *White Poverty: How Exposing Myths about Race and Class Can Reconstruct America*, in which he spoke about the "Southern Strategy," employed by the USA Republican Party beginning in the 1960s whose goal was to gain power by promoting division based on race. The strategy involved seeing people of color and immigrants as threats to white persons in terms of economics, employment, self-esteem, and political influence. Based on a scarcity consciousness, any gain in civil rights or economic well-being by African Americans was viewed as a threat to the economic status of whites. In today's vitriolic political environment, dominated by isolation and scarcity thinking, every immigrant is perceived a threat to white peoples' jobs, despite the fact that undocumented residents initially do work that most American citizens choose to avoid. A theology of unity and abundance, grounded in Franciscan and Whiteheadian spirituality, seeks to unite persons of all races to eliminate poverty

---

14 Thomas Merton, *Essential Writings*, edited by Christine M. Bochen (Maryknoll, NY: Orbis Books), 90.

and improve the economic, educational, and medical well-being of all people. This is a spiritual issue not just political. It shapes how we see the world and our own lives. In this spirit, expand your sense of unity to embrace the political and economic sphere. Affirming that "there is no other," connect your overall well-being with the overall well-being of the Earth's and our nation's most vulnerable people. Ask for divine guidance in discovering ways to partner with economically vulnerable people to enhance their lives. This may involve advocating for a minimum standard of living, universal health care, better schools, raising taxes on the wealthiest to support the most disadvantaged, and exploring the relationship between economic and ecological justice. This may mean challenging race based political policies that make voting more difficult or policies that promote the denial of basic human rights to immigrants.

Remembering that "peace is the way," experience your unity of spirit with those whom you see as the perpetrators of injustice as well as those who are manipulated by power hungry politicians. Seek to be a healer as well as a prophet.

Peace is Every Step. In light of Francis' outreach to a Muslim sultan and Whitehead's appreciation of Buddhism, it would be remiss not to bring in the wisdom of spiritual leaders of other faith traditions. A Vietnamese Buddhist monk says that "peace is every step." Calm quiet breathing and intentional walking restore our equanimity and connection with the planet.

In this exercise, take a walk with contemplative intentionality. Breathe gently and deeply. Notice your spiritual and emotional state. Breathe out any fear, anxiety, and anger, recognizing that these are passing states. You can let go of negative and alienating emotions and experience your loving connection with all life. Breathe in the beauty of the earth. Breathe in your connection with all creation. Breathe in your intimacy with divine love.

7
TRAGIC BEAUTY

MAKING PEACE WITH DEATH AND LIMITATION

*Praised be You, my God, through our sister Bodily Death,
from whom no one can escape.
How dreadful for those who die in sin,
How lovely for those who are found in Your Most Holy Will,
For the second death can do them no harm.*[15]

At the heart of the nature of things, there are always the dream of youth and the harvest of tragedy. The Adventure of the Universe starts with the dream and reaps Tragic Beauty. This is the secret of the union of Zest with Peace: - That the suffering attains its end in a Harmony of Harmonies. The immediate experience of this Final Fact, with its union of Youth and Tragedy, is the sense of Peace. In this way the world receives its persuasion toward such perfections as are possible for its diverse individual occasions.[16]

---

15 Murray Bodo, *The Journey and the Dream*, 169-170.
16 Alfred North Whitehead, *Adventures of Ideas*, 296.

Martin Luther once asserted that "in the midst of life, we are surrounded by death." Death, and the denial of death, is a reality that shapes the decision-making and attitudes of persons and nations and touches every aspect of our lives. Death is the one reality that no creature can avoid. All things must pass, and that includes our lives, the lives of loved ones, and that of our nation. Empires come and go. Athens, Babylon, Assyria, and Rome are ancient history. Great Britain no longer rules the seas, and the American Empire is crumbling as is the white male domination of our nation. Even the planet is mortal and will one day disappear, engulfed by a luminous solar explosion.

The reality of death, grounded in the primordial reality of process and change, can lead to the attempt to halt the movement of time and change through violence and hate. We can, like today's white Christian nationalists, choose to burn down the house just to maintain our superiority over immigrants, the LGBTQ+ community, and persons of color. Ruled by fear of losing what we have or returning to an idealized (and non-existent) past, we abandon Jesus to follow authoritarian leaders motivated by hate and power, whom we perceived to be saviors and protectors of our privilege and power. Yet, the pandemic as well as our personal mortality reveals the deep secret, the mortality rate is 100% and most likely will remain so for persons and planets. This reality can deaden our spirits or awaken us to the beauty of this good earth and the lives of those around us. We can seek retribution, or we can delight in a world of praise. The perpetually perishing nature of life can provoke wonder as well as fear, and creativity as well as destruction.

In my early seventies and a grateful member of the Medicare generation, I feel the realities of diminishment and death on a daily basis. Perhaps you do too. Beyond my personal anxieties, I also struggle with the reality of climate change and the threat of environmental and civilizational collapse. These realities can plunge us into depression, denial, and destruction, or they can invite us to proclaim with each new morning, "This is the day that God has made, and I will rejoice and be glad in it." One of my favorite authors William Saroyan notes, that "one day in the afternoon of the world, glum death will come and sit in you, and when you get up to walk, you will be as glum as death, but if you're lucky, this will only make the fun better and the love greater." While recognizing the ubiquity of death, reflected in plagues, war, and in his own chronic physical ailments, Luther maintains hope in the mighty fortress of God's love, "In the midst of death, we are surrounded by life." This is the day, this is the moment, when we can experience peace, wholeness, community, and harmony with all nature. The perpetually perishing world can invite us to love, adventure, and healing; to embrace the healing movements of the ever-moving God.

The reality of death shaped Francis' and Whitehead's vision of theology and spirituality. Francis was well aware of the brevity of life. Francis witnessed the crusades, wars between city states, and lives cut short by disease. Francis was wounded in battle and during his recuperation experienced his first inclination toward a transformed way of life. In his later years, Francis lived with chronic and debilitating illness. Yet, despite his daily encounters with death, in a time in which Francis experienced almost unendurable physical pain, Francis penned his most enduring words, "The Canticle of the Sun," or "Canticle of the Creatures." Beauty abounds and praise inspires despite life's tragedies. Even at death's door, he experienced God's healing presence, and could sing "Hallelujah" with trust that God who had called him to Holy Poverty, oneness with the human and non-human world, and vocation to repair the church and the world, would be his companion in suffering as well as joy:

> Praised be You, my God, through our sister Bodily Death,
> from whom no one can escape.
> How dreadful for those who die in sin,
> How lovely for those who are found in Your Most Holy Will,

For the second death can do them no harm.[17]

While the words of the third line of Francis' hymn to God at the descending edges of life initially appear ominous, and reflect the orthodoxy of his times, I believe his intent is not to threaten people with hell and damnation but to say that the fear and denial of death bring sorrow and dread, while trust in God in the midst of change enables us to find beauty even in our final moments. Even at death's door, we can cherish the beauties of the earth, knowing we are a part of God's circle of love, whose center is everywhere and whose circumference is nowhere. There is a pathway to find peace as you walk through the valley of the shadow of death and that pathway is praise, the virtue that connects us with God and the goodness of the Earth and its creatures.

Whitehead once asserted that the greatest evil of life is to be found in the fact that the past fades, the present is fleeting, and life is a process of perpetual perishing. All things must pass and with Gautama Buddha, Whitehead recognized that clinging to what must perish is the source of pain, regret, and I would add greed and violence. Whitehead felt the searing pain of his son's death in World War I. I suspect that his son's death inspired him to focus on the enduring realities of life and affirm the significance of spirituality and theology as sources of both consolation and adventure. Aware of the fragility of life, Whitehead proclaimed that all things are treasured in the consequent nature of God. God's ever expansive and infinitely intimate memory enables us to live courageously and ethically knowing that our lives make a difference to God and to the world beyond ourselves. The impact of our decisions, positive and negative, and our kindness and commitment to heal the world, lives on in God's tender care that nothing be lost and God's artistic and salvific transformation of the wreckage of life into possibilities for healing and wholeness.

In reflection on the spirituality of Whitehead and the parents of the Franciscan movement, we discover the life-changing insight

---

17 Murray Bodo, *The Journey and the Dream*, 169-170.

that when there cannot be a cure, there can be a healing, and that even if our efforts to heal the world fail, we can find joy in each moment's companionship with God and our neighbors. Simple acts of love, such as embracing a person with leprosy or providing spiritual counsel to a wolf or entrusting the lives of those we love to God's care, heal the world one encounter at a time. We are, as Blessed Mother Teresa says, called to be faithful even if we are not successful. Even if we are not cured of a chronic or life-threatening illness, or the lifelong dark night of the soul Mother Teresa experienced or life's problems continue to remain unfixable, we can experience a healing and the peace that passes understanding. Embracing the perpetual perishing of life and the reality of our personal and planetary finitude, we can nevertheless moment by moment do something beautiful for God, knowing that God treasures our lives and that in life and death, God is our companion, guide, and support.

FRANCIS' FAITH: FACING DEATH AND PRAISING GOD

Francis spent his final years in declining health. Perhaps, his peregrinations had worn down his body as a result of his constant pilgrimage and fasting. Yet as the apostle Paul counsels, "So we do not lose heart. Even though our outer nature is wasting away, our inner nature is being renewed day by day." (2 Corinthians 4;16) The Divine Companion who called Francis to repair the church, opened his eyes to holiness in lepers, inspired him to cross political boundaries, and claim sparrows and wolves as kin, renewed and repaired his spirit despite his failing body. Even in his final days, Francis was, as biographer Thomas of Celeno asserts, "always new, always fresh, always beginning again."

When his physician declared that death was imminent, Francis lifted his hands to the heavens and cried out, "Welcome sister Death!" Then Francis asked his faithful companions, Brother Angelo and Brother Leo to chant the words of the Canticle of the Creatures. As they concluded the Canticle, Francis composed another verse that bears repeating as counsel to us today, that can be summarized with "Praised by You, my God, through our sister Bodily Death." Francis and his companions joyfully chanted this hymn throughout his final days as a reminder that nothing in life and death can separate from the love of God. (Romans 8:38-39) Connected with God and one another, we can experience a lively death, while isolated self-centered individualism leads to a deathful life. Francis recognized that death was open door to eternity. Death also united him with all who suffer. Solidarity with suffering, he believed, is the pathway to personal and global healing.

To some of Francis' monastic colleagues, his deathbed hymn of praise seemed inappropriate behavior by a holy man. They were like one of the saints of the Cape Cod church that I pastored, who asked "Why are you so joyful when you celebrate communion? Aren't we supposed to be solemn and reflective?" I responded, "You're right. We need to ponder Jesus' last supper and the Cross on Calvary. We also need to rejoice in God's love for us and proclaim that Christ is Risen and we will rise, too!" In like fashion, Brother Elias challenged Francis' deathbed joy: "In this city where people view you as a saint, I fear lest they be scandalized in seeing you prepare for death in this way?" Though racked with pain, Francis responded, "For in spite of all that I endure, I feel so close to God that I cannot help singing." True to his experience of God as his closest companion, Francis died with words of praise on his lips. Legend has it that as the saint breathed his last, a flock of larks alighted on the monastery roof and began chanting in their own hymns of praise, joining their own grief with gratitude for God's presence in Francis' life.

When I ponder Francis' dying days, I am reminded of the nineteenth century hymn, penned by Robert Lowry (1826-1899) and popularized by the Irish singer-songwriter Enya. Noted earlier in this book, this hymn reflects the hopeful optimism of Whiteheadian and Franciscan theology: threat is real, death is universal, and yet this holy moment can connect us with God and lives forever in God's everlasting and evolving memory.

> My life flows on in endless song
> Above earth's lamentation.
> I hear the real, though far off hymn
> That hails the new creation
> Above the tumult and the strife,
> I hear the music ringing;
> It sounds an echo in my soul
> How can I keep from singing?
>
> What through the tempest loudly roars,
> I hear the truth, it live'th.
> What through the darkness round me close,
> Songs in the night it give'th.
>
> No storm can shake my inmost calm
> While to that rock I'm clinging.
> Since love is lord of Heaven and earth
> How can I keep from singing?
> How can I keep from singing?

Deep faith is political as well as personal. Trust in the goodness of the universe enables us to experience joy amid turmoil and compassion amid chaos. Ninety years after Lowry penned his lyrics, Doris Plenn (1909-1991) added a stanza and shared it with a family friend, the famed singer songwriter Pete Seeger (1919-2014), who popularized it as a protest against the anti-democratic tactics of 1950's McCarthy era. These additional words provide solace and courage for those who face the anti-democratic, socially divisive, and planet destroying politics of our time. Political and religious tyrants may appear to have the upper hand, but their power will dissipate, and their idolatry will be unmasked. The humble power of a Loving God and loving communities outlasts even the most diabolical politicians.

When tyrants tremble, sick with fear,
And hear their death-knell ringing,
When friends rejoice both far and near,
How can I keep from singing?

Francis knew, as did Lowry and Plenn, that God is our faithful companion inviting us to solidarity with others in times of pain and crisis. How can we keep from singing!

I suspect Francis was buoyed at his time of death by his mystical experience on Mount Alverna just two years before his death. Meditating on Christ's Passion, Bonaventure reports that "the man filled with God understood that just as he imitated Christ in the actions of his life, so he should be conformed to him in the affliction and sorrow of his passion, before he would pass out of this world." Shortly thereafter, Francis had a vision of six Seraphs surrounded the Crucified Christ. Francis felt Jesus' pain as well as Jesus' solidarity and love for our suffering world. Francis realized that Christ's suffering and immortality were one reality. God is the Great Empath. Francis so identified with Jesus' suffering and solidarity that Jesus' own wounds, the stigmata, appeared on his own body.

While we may struggle with the image of Francis' stigmata and be tempted to see it as some form of self-flagellation, I believe that Francis' mystical experience of Jesus' suffering points to the humility of God and our own call to see our own suffering as a call to heal the sick, release the captives, and seek liberty for the oppressed. As our hearts expand, we feel the heartbeat of the Great Empath in every beat of our own hearts. The fellow sufferer who understands calls us to healthy identification and action in response to the world's pain. Pain is unavoidable for those with open hearts, and so is joy and gratitude.

Francis could face diminishment with peace because he experienced the peace that passes all understanding, the peace that comes from letting go of the individual self and identifying with the God's Fountain of Love flowing through our lives and all things, joining us with the Ever-flowing Self of the Universe.

Sickness, death, and persecution do not release us from our obligations to God and our neighbors. Indeed, the struggles of life, while not intended by God, can be refined by the one who works for good in all things. (Romans 8:28) From his experience in a German concentration camp, Viktor Frankl counsels that "Everything can be taken from a man but one thing: the last of the human freedoms—to choose one's attitude in any given set of circumstances, to choose one's own way." Jesus went to the Cross a free person, liberated from the bondage of isolated selfhood and self-interest. Joined with the Soul of the Universe, the Cosmic Christ/Jesus, embodied in the historical Jesus, pronounced forgiveness on those who persecuted him. The way of the cross, as Dietrich Bonhoeffer avers, became the way of life for Jesus, Francis, Clare, Bonaventure, and for us.

In our tumultuous time, death is all around us. We are confronted with our personal mortality, the death of species, the melting of ice bergs, and the death of coral reefs. We can give up hope in the wake of our planet's fragility. There is no guarantee that we can save the planet from global climate change or our nation from the powers of incivility, divisiveness, and destruction of democracy. Although our lives are perpetually perishing, we can join God in the quest to heal the Earth one act at a time. We can be faithful to the One who sings in melodies of sparrows and howls with wolves and inspires every act of kindness. Then we can, with the apostle Paul, see a larger vision of the world and ourselves in which death is a portal to divine love, inspiring us to give thanks even for Sister Death:

> O death, where is thy sting?
> O grave, where is thy victory?
> But thanks be to God, which giveth us the victory
> through our Lord Jesus Christ. (1 Corinthians 15:55, 57)

Our victory will be the gift of lovingkindness and not the exhibition of power. With Francis, we will experience a Fountain of Light and Love flowing through us and see ourselves as unique, unrepeatable, and immortal drops in God's River of Love, who by our lives can be God's companions in preserving our world of praise.

WHITEHEAD'S VISION OF TRAGIC BEAUTY AND HOLY ADVENTURE

Whitehead asserts that reality can be described in terms of the two contrasting intuitions: flux and permanence. All things flow and nothing remains the same. Like sands of an hourglass so are the days of our lives, as a soap opera motto asserts. One moment, we are children at play bounding down the stairs and in a blink of an eye, we are applying for US Social Security and Medicare and holding on to the rail as we descend the staircase. "The flux of things is one ultimate generalization around which we must weave our philosophical system," not to mention our brief and sometimes conflictual lives.

In contrast to the constantly flowing river of time, there is a sense of timelessness that we can on special days feel as we gaze at the heavens or delight in our own ethereal uniqueness of spirit. When we feel the immediacy of a childhood experience, and once again take a flight of imagination, or feel unity with the universe as we marvel at a star-filled night, we feel the eternity and timelessness of the spirit. There are no boundaries when our spirits are aligned with God's everlasting and ever-evolving imagination. We are no longer solely defined as members of the Medicare generation; we are companions with the never-changing, ever-changing One, embodying time as the moving image of eternity. Whitehead also describes "the permanences of things – the solid earth, the mountains, the stones, the Egyptian Pyramids, the spirit of man,

God."[1] The interplay of changelessness and change is described in the words of a hymn from Whitehead's and my childhood:

> Abide with me;
> Fast falls the eventide.

Whitehead notes that "the ultimate evil in the temporal world is deeper than any specific evil. It lies in the fact that the past fades, that time is a 'perpetual perishing,'" As the hymn says, "Fast falls the eventide." And then the lyricist laments,

> Swift to its close ebbs out life's little day;
> Earth's joys grow dim, its glories pass away;
> Change and decay in all around I see.[2]

Perhaps reflecting on his own personal losses, the atrocities of war, and the passage of his own life, Whitehead asks, "Why should there be novelty without loss of this direct unison of immediacy of things?"[3] The process is the reality, and change is good. Flux is essential for growth and transformation, and the realization of human adventure. Without change, there would be no hope for progress or justice in the social order. Then again, change can bring loss and grief. Global and national change can provoke anger and alienation as we see in the rise of white Christian nationalism and anti-immigrant feeling in the United States. We cannot halt the process of change whether in our personal lives, national demographics, or the affairs of nations. The challenge in facing life's inevitable change is to find something healthy that "abides" in the midst of change, inspiring us to embrace change with acceptance, vision, purpose, and agency. As the lyricist concludes, "…in life, in death, O God, abide with me."

The greatest change we experience is death: our own deaths, the deaths of loved ones, and the death of the institutions we prize and upon which we depend. The reality of death can be a liber-

---

1   Alfred North Whitehead, *Process and Reality,* 208.
2   Henry Lyte, "Abide with Me." (1847)
3   Alfred North Whitehead, 208.

ating call to adventure and an invitation to rejoice in each unique and unrepeatable moment. It also can promote anxiety and fear as well as greed, violence, and clinging to the status quo, the way things were, and the old-time religion or a national "golden age." We must move forward to respond creatively to the changes in our lives, and at the same time, treasure the gifts of past experience and tradition. To reiterate, the reality of change is a political and planetary as well as personal and relational issue: similar to our own experiences of being intellectually, relationally, and emotionally stuck, the current political crisis in the USA and other nations is the result of our personal and corporate inability to face change constructively and our unwillingness to look beyond self-interest to embrace world loyalty and the well-being of future generations. Conservative politicians, religious leaders, and their followers recognize the threat of change to the status quo of white patriarchal dominance and "traditional" Christian values, and want to turn back the clock, despite their economic and personal dependence on the very technologies that promote rapid change: internet, social media, economic capitalism, and ease of travel. The river flows and we can either go with the flow, exerting our agency to shape the contours of the moving future, or be drowned in our attempts to turn back the flow of life.

Eight centuries after Francis and his spiritual companions faced changes in their world, we need to discover life-supporting ways to respond to change. In the world of process and perpetual perishing, does Whitehead provide a healthy and creative answer to death? Can we come to see God's healing presence in sickness, aging, and death? Can we chant praises to Sister Death at the descending edges of life? Can we see change and the loss that comes with death as a call to adventure rather than a threat to the status quo? Can we rejoice in this moment's beauty despite the uncertainty of the future?

Whitehead notes three responses organisms make to radical changes in their environment, whether those changes involve sickness, death, age, violence, demographics, politics, or war and peace. Whitehead's list is not exhaustive, but it describes a broad spectrum of personal and institutional responses to life's perpetual perishing. For many organisms and communities, the most common response to change is to *deny* its reality, treating the stark realities of change and threat as if they don't exist. In Leo Tolstoy's spiritual classic, *The Death of Ivan Ilych,* the protagonist Ivan Ilych can't initially imagine that he is dying. He believes that it's normal for others to die, including the mortal Socrates from the famous syllogism, but death is an impossibility for him. Others may die, but how can his unique experience as Ivan disappear from the face of the earth? Despite the obvious symptoms of life-threatening illness, Ivan returns to work, believing that as long as he works, he can banish death. His denial, like all denial, eventually ends in failure as pain intrudes on his workday and plunges Ilych into further depression.

Virtually all of us live with some form of denial either personally or institutionally. Despite the clear evidence of the reality climate change, millions of Christians, entranced by their belief in the elusive second coming, the spoils of capitalism, and the bloviations of prevaricating politicians, deny the threat of climate change because it conflicts with their theological viewpoint that God is in control of history and God will decide unilaterally what happens to our planet. They believe that God – or American ingenuity – will save us regardless of what happens to our planet. Life can go on as usual until Jesus comes again in destruction and glory. The more cynical among us, upon observing the rhetoric of politicians who chant "drill, drill, drill," believe that even among faithful Christians, climate denial is grounded in self-interest and greed and the quest to make as large a profit as possible despite the dangers to future generations. Eventually, however, denial is unsustainable. The cancer returns. Addiction destroys our health and relationships. Failure to follow good health practices contributes to a personal health crisis. The seas rise, weather patterns change, famines lead to immigration by millions, catastrophic storms and forest fires become the norm, and if we persist in denial, we will be unprepared to respond to change in a constructive way. The handwriting is on the wall and it spells doom for our civilization and reality, revealing the theological and ethical bankruptcy of conservative religious movements and their narrow understandings of salvation.

Another dysfunctional way organisms respond to radical change is through an overwhelming sense of helplessness. When his denial is pierced, Ivan Ilych comes to see death as the only reality, before which he has no agency or ability for change. Whitehead describes this response in terms of "acute disruption," in which the perceived threat is so great in our estimation, and our resources so small, that we abandon agency and possibility.[4] Only the threat exists, and before it, we are powerless. We have no inner or communal responses to the reality of change. The diagnosis of cancer may be seen as a death sentence, and we prepare to die even though we still have options to increase our lifespan and live meaningful lives despite the shadow of mortality. Seeing ourselves as victims of fate or the influence of the past, we give up hope and passively await the inevitable. We can neither change ourselves nor do we have the resources to become agents of our destiny despite external circumstances of family of origin, institutional injustice, or illness. As a pastor and chaplain, I have observed persons giving up in the face of life-threatening illness, sedating or narcotizing themselves with alcohol and drugs until the final moment.

We can see helplessness and hopelessness in the political arena as well as in personal decision-making. The impact of hopelessness is felt by both liberals and conservatives. I often hear people say, "The problems are too big. There's nothing I can do about it" "My vote doesn't matter," or "I've given up on politics, nothing will change. They're all alike." Dominated by feelings of passivity and defeat, we believe that larger powers, whether God, fate, big government, or institutional evil, are in control and the best we can do is keep our heads down, live our lives, and stay out of the way. Hopelessness and powerlessness, like denial, leave the future

---

4   Alfred North Whitehead, *Adventures of Ideas*, 259.

in the hands of our greatest fears or in the machinations of political leaders whom we trust to set things right, defeat our foes, and return us to the good old days of privilege and power. At such moments, we need to be reminded that we have agency and that our decisions matter. We need to be freed from our dependence on faux saviors and awaken to the saving power of actions motivated by a commitment to humility, interdependence, and sacrificial living. As an antidote to the destructive impact of denial, hopelessness, and reliance on false messiahs, we need a restored sense of trust in what is truly ultimate in love and companionship. "In life, in death, O Lord, abide with me," as the hymn, invoked by Whitehead, affirms. We need to recognize that even the smallest act can transform the world. A butterfly flapping its wings, an act of kindness, the willingness to change, can be catalysts that give birth to creative transformation of our lives and our institutions. When we doubt our everyday actions matter, let us remember the fragile firefly and commit to healing the Earth one act at a time. "This little light of mine, I'm gonna let it shine!" we affirm in the face of that threatens us.

Mother Teresa asserted that our task is not to be successful but faithful. We must be God's healing companions regardless of the outcome. We must recognize that there is "life after doom," as Brian McLaren states. In the recognition that we can make a difference one loving and compassion action at a time, we reclaim our agency and realistic hope. We cannot claim that victory is assured whether in a presidential election, protecting democracy, or responding successfully to climate change, but we can pray in the words of Harry Emerson Fosdick's hymn, "save us from weak resignation to the evils we deplore." We are not alone. Amid the threats we experience, the still small voice of God speaks in our spirits and invites us to peace and power amid the storm. In the storms of life, Jesus is quietly in the boat with us, and though the storms rage and our boat tosses to and fro, we will not drown. We can see the other shore and pick up our oar. Trusting God's gentle presence and guidance, we can be God's agents of creative transformation.

Denial and hopeless resignation are spiritual attitudes that encourage passivity in response to the crises we face, whether these involve global threats such as climate change or personal crises such as chronic and life-threatening illness and personal mortality. In contrast to these passive responses, Whitehead suggests another path, the one I have been describing, the way of creative transformation, reflecting our commitment to initiate novelty to match the novelties of our environment and personal lives In the spirit of psychiatrist and Holocaust survivor, Viktor Frankl, while we can't control the events of our lives, we have the ability to respond with creativity and compassion and in choosing to be agents in times of crisis, we nurture our own personal healing and contribute to healing the world. This is the way of self-transcendence Whitehead identifies with peace. Yet, far from being passive, self-transcendence awakens us to inner resources and alternative possibilities that enable us to experience healing even when there is little likelihood of a cure. The novelty, disruptive in nature, which once anesthetized and overwhelmed us is transformed into an invitation to creativity and artistry, to choosing life rather than accepting death and seeing ourselves as agents of our destiny, who work to change a world in which there are no ultimate promises of success. We can choose, even in small ways, to be poets and artists of our lives and our planet in imitation of the Poet of the Universe.

Creative transformation involves a commitment to grow in wisdom and stature and to accept and embrace our current situation as the pathway to new possibilities for spiritual growth and responsible action. Whitehead asserts that within life's limitations, we can discover a womb of possibility. God's aim in each moment of experience is the best for that impasse. In terms of the ideal world, the best may initially seem bad as Whitehead notes. For example, we may have to radically simplify our lifestyle and sacrifice our economic privilege. In our own lives, there is often a great distance between the actual and the ideal. Negative events, or the critique of others, often reveal where we have gone astray or failed to care for ourselves or others. But, leaning toward God's vision one step at a time widens the horizons of possibility and agency.

Going beyond denial and hopelessness, we gain a more accurate understanding of our situation. We discover that the diagnosis of cancer does not define us. Yes, we have a life-threatening illness or a traumatic past and we also have choices, gifts, and interests that also define us. The threat of death and the reality of past injustice, violence, trauma, and pain are real and must be addressed medically, spiritually, emotionally, psychologically, and, in certain cases, politically and through the justice system. Yet, in this moment of tragic beauty, there is also the call forward of adventure and healing. "This is the day that God has made and I will rejoice and be glad in it," and for as long as I have breath, I can experience and add to the beauty of the universe. The spiritual, moral, and healing arcs are at work in our lives and lead us to live creatively with what we cannot change and act courageously in response to what we can change.

Creative transformation is the gift of a wider vision and a greater sense of self in which I discover that I am not alone. I am one with the universe, connected to creation, and sustained by God's energy of love. Our sense of self is no longer defined by individualism or isolation, or our precarious health condition, but by our relationships with God and the world around us in all its wonder, beauty, and tragedy. The small, frightened self has expanded to embrace the Self of the Universe, the fellow sufferer who understands and the joyful companion who celebrates. We discover that our story is part of a much larger story, the story of the universe, and the Fountain of Love which joins the Infinite and infinitesimal. In all the changes of life, we can affirm that the Living God is our companion, energizing, enlightening, empowering, and embracing. God is at work in our lives, providing a way forward where we previously perceived no way ahead. God treasures our lives eternally. We all will eventually perish but we live forevermore in God's all-embracing, all-healing memory.

> The steadfast love of God never ceases,
>   God's mercies never come to an end;
> they are new every morning;
>   great is your faithfulness.
> "God is my portion," says my soul,
>   "therefore I will hope in God." (Lamentations 3:22-24)

In the spirit of Franciscan theology, Whitehead affirms that God is our portion and hope. Our hope is in God's love for us, our impact on God and the world, and the image of ongoing companionship moment by moment and beyond the grave in God's Holy Adventure. We can run the race with hope, knowing that though our lives perish, in God, they live forevermore and will be the foundation of God's healing and transforming movements in the world beyond us. As I've said to the children – and adults – of congregations where I served as pastor, "God loves you, we love you, you matter, and you can do something beautiful for God." Moreover, in God's everlasting energy of love and all-encompassing memory, "nothing in life and death can separate us from the love of God." Even as we face our deaths, sometimes fearfully and anxiously, God is near and even then, we can say "Praise God. Thank you for this one wondrous, wild, and beautiful life."

SPIRITUAL PRACTICES FOR GLOBAL HEALERS

Divine creativity calls us to self-creativity and agency. Divine humility challenges us to face life's struggles recognizing both our strength and weakness. Healthy spirituality calls us to be persons of stature who recognize our limits and discover possibility within the limitations of life. Whitehead and the Franciscan spiritual parents saw beauty in tragedy and agency within limitation. Our humility inspires us to accept our morality and embrace everlasting values that call us to new horizons.

Living with the Serenity Prayer. North American theology Reinhold Niebuhr's (1892-1971) Serenity Prayer has been central to twelve step movements and a guidepost for persons facing unavoidable limits. It bears repeating as a source of consolation and inspiration to agency. I regularly use the original and longer version of the Serenity Prayer to enable me to find peace in the storms of life. Yet serenity inspires agency and the choice to claim my power to right the wrongs I observe. While not directly inspired by Franciscan spirituality or Whitehead's philosophy, the Serenity Prayer embraces the interplay of acceptance and agency characteristic of their vision of reality and human creativity and responsibility. It also echoes the counsel of Viktor Frankl, "When we are no longer able to change a situation, we are challenged to change ourselves," and as a contemporary addition of the prayer counsels, to "change the things I cannot accept."

> God grant me the serenity
> to accept the things I cannot change;
> courage to change the things I can;
> and wisdom to know the difference.
>
> Living one day at a time;
> enjoying one moment at a time;
> accepting hardships as the pathway to peace;
> taking, as He did, this sinful world
> as it is, not as I would have it;
> trusting that He will make all things right
> if I surrender to His Will;
> that I may be reasonably happy in this life
> and supremely happy with Him
> forever in the next.
> Amen.

Similar to my counsel on the Prayer of St. Francis, I invite you to read this prayer each morning, meditating on its meaning in your life, carry a card with the shorter or longer version to consult during the day, and remember the prayer as a way of restoring both your equanimity and agency when you are prone to be anxious, impatient, and complacent at life's circumstances. In times of confusion or challenge, we can pray, "God give me serenity to follow your vision to change the world one moment at a time."

Living a Life of Stature. The experience of peace with life's "unfixables" such as death and diminishment involves the experience of self-transcendence.[5] Self-transcendence is the gift of perspective in which our selves are perceived as part of a larger universe which embraces and transcends us, the experience of the interplay of the Infinite and the infinitesimal. Psalm 8 captures this contrast:

> When I look at your heavens, the work of your fingers,
>   the moon and the stars that you have established;
> what are humans that you are mindful of them,
>   mortals that you care for them?
> Yet you have made them a little lower than God
>   and crowned them with glory and honor. (Psalm 8:3-5)

In speaking of the quest for largeness of spirit, process theologian and my Claremont professor Bernard Loomer (1912-1985) describe the experience of size or stature. Loomer's words also bear repeating on a regular basis and in this text as the inspiration to a spirituality that embraces both beauty and tragedy and health and illness and all the other polarities of life. I read these words of Loomer a few times each month as part of my spiritual inventory and inspiration of my own quest to grow in Wisdom and Stature and openness to God's call of adventure. Sometimes, in challenging times, I simply say "God, give me stature" just as I repeat "God make me an instrument of your peace." In internalizing these words, I have been inspired to embrace otherness in all its diversity, personal and political, with compassion and welcome change as God's call to new horizons and novel adventures.

> By S-I-Z-E I mean the stature of a person's soul, the range and depth of his love, his capacity for relationships. I mean the volume of life you can take into your being and still maintain your integrity and individuality, the intensity and variety of outlook you can entertain in the unity of your being

---

5 A phrase coined by Episcopalian spiritual guide Alan Jones.

without feeling defensive or insecure. I mean the strength of your spirit to encourage others to become freer in the development of their diversity and uniqueness. I mean the power to sustain more complex and enriching tensions. I mean the magnanimity of concern to provide conditions that enable others to increase in stature.[6]

In this spiritual practice, I invite you to ponder the "heavens above" or photographs from the Hubble or Webb telescopes. Reflect on the immensity of the universe and the finitude of our small planet and lifespans. How great the universe and its Creative Wisdom are!

Now consider that you are intimately connected with the totality of the universe and God such that the boundaries between the Infinite are erased, and you experience yourself, as Emily Dickinson says, as a finite infinity . As poet Max Ehrman asserts in his poem Desiderata: "You are a child of the universe, no less than the trees and the stars; you have a right to be here." You participate in the Divine Infinity. Your unique life is treasured eternally in God's experience. The whole energy of the universe, God's fountain of life flows in and through you, and finite as you are you are also Infinite in God's love. Joined and God to the universe, "there is no other." See yourself as connected with everyone you meet and creation in its wondrous diversity.

You may also choose to reflect on your vision of survival after death. What images of everlasting life inspire you? In what ways will you live on after your death? How will your life go on, either in impact or continued personal adventures? Give thanks for the opportunity to share in the Infinity of God and God's creation.

---

6   Loomer, Bernard M., "S-I-Z-E. is the Measure," *Religious Experience and Process Theology*, ed. Harry James Cargas and Bernard Lee (New York: Paulist Press, 1976), pp. 69-76

8

WE ARE THE ONES WE'VE BEEN WAITING FOR

REFLECTIONS ON THE NEW FRANCIS

In her Poem for South African Women, June Jordan asks, "who will join this standing up" against apartheid and injustice, and then responds, "we are the ones we have been waiting for." We live in a perilous time, the best and worst of times, and each day we are confronted with choices about climate change, human rights, the future of future of democracy, immigration, and our own relational and spiritual well-being. In words penned by Harry Emerson Fosdick in the interim between two world wars, a great depression, and the realities of poverty and racism, we hear the call to face the hour in which we live.

> Lo the hosts of evil round us, scorn the Christ,
> assail his ways.
> From the fears that long have bound us,
> free our hearts to faith and praise.
> Grant us wisdom, grant us courage,
> for the living of these days.[1]

We need the wisdom of the ages, embodied by spiritual, theological, and philosophical sages, who faced the crises of their time: poverty and crusade, religious schism, global warfare, sexism, and

[1] Harry Emerson Fosdick, "God of Grace and God of Glory." (1930)

racism, with vision, courage, and openness. In looking to theologians, philosophers. and spiritual guides of wisdom and stature, we find our own path toward spiritual and planetary transformation. We find vision, courage, and inspiration for our vocations in our season of the human adventure. Teilhard de Chardin once commented that "we are the new Francis" in our vocation of building the earth and joining God in the process of incarnating Christ in the evolutionary process. Honoring our own insights and creativity, our own empathy and restless quest for justice, we can incarnate the spirit of Francis, Clare, Bonaventure, and Whitehead "for the living of these days."

Throughout my theological adventures as a pastor, professor, seminary administrator, and spiritual guide, I have asserted that holistic theology and spirituality joins the sacred synthesis of vision, promise, and practice: an imaginative and insightful description of God's presence in our lives, relationships, communities, and the universe; a promise that we can embody the vision we affirm; and practices that enable us nurture vision and vocation in our lives.

Though separated by seven centuries, religious tradition, technology, scientific understandings, and political context, Whitehead, Francis, Clare, and Bonaventure are kindred visionaries who share the vision of a lively, dynamic, relational world of praise. They affirm that the universe is alive in every nook and cranny. Our souls and cells reflect the flowing fountain of God's Light and Wisdom, energizing and inspiring us with each new moment and over the long haul of history. Long before the birth of the environmental movement, the Franciscan spiritual guides recognized the sacredness and vitality of each created thing. They saw connections between every creature and its environment and recognized that humans and non-humans are bound together in an intricate web of relationships. Sparrows can listen to sermons and wolves can receive ethical counsel. Worms yearn for safety and rabbits resist capture. More amazing, we humans can humbly learn from and communicate with our non-human kin! With

Whitehead, the Franciscan parents visualize nature alive with beauty, intentionality, and experience. Accordingly, humankind's vocation is to live in harmony with the non-human world, living as simply and reverentially as possible.

Whitehead, Francis, Clare, and Bonaventure portray a God filled universe. In Whitehead's case, the world lives by the incarnation of God. God comes to us humbly as the source of ideals for each moment of experience. God does not demand or coerce but works within our lives calling us forward toward horizons of truth, beauty, and goodness, relating to every aspect of our lives and citizenship. For the Franciscan parents, the image of a world of praise points to God's presence within each creature, urging it to be in sync with its Wise Creator and its human and non-human kin. God is humbly at work in every existing thing inspiring all creation to praise, not out of fear, but in response to God's loving wisdom.

God inspires us in every moment of experience: in Francis' call to repair the church at San Damiano and later his embodiment of Christ's suffering for humanity at Alverna; in Clare's restless spirit, questioning of her culture's values, and vision of women's spiritual empowerment; in Bonaventure's experience of Francis' mystical stigmata; and Whitehead's identification of philosophy as mystical and emerging from our deepest, often unspoken, encounters with the Holy. Following the way of the humble, suffering Jesus, Francis, Clare, Bonaventure, and Whitehead, promise that those who seek will find and that persons can experience God's vision in the dynamic, interdependent, experiential, and innovative realities of their lives.

While Whitehead does not provide a list of spiritual practices, his philosophical vision is grounded in the intentional interplay of reason, reflection, observation, solitude, and community. Whitehead counsels us to question static and authoritarian dogmas; to live by love and reconciliation and not fear and hate; to treasure the inherent value of the human and non-human world; to expand our vision beyond parochialism to cosmopolitanism; and to transfer our loyalties from self-interest to world loyalty. Whitehead invites us to imagine God touching our bodies, minds, and spirits with ideals and possibilities and challenging us to embody these in our daily lives. Whitehead also teaches us to affirm that our lives matter to others, to our communities, to our nation, to our planet, and to God. God treasures our lives in their joy and sorrow and, in the challenges of the living of our days, our calling is to do something beautiful for God and our earthly kin. What we do in this moment may perish in its immediacy, but it lives evermore in God's memory and adds to or detracts from God's quest for truth, beauty, goodness, peace, and justice, Shalom in our world. Knowing God is with us, we can move from cramped self-interest to spacious world loyalty in which all creation is kin, and our lives go on in endless love despite life's lamentations. We can identify our self with the Self of the Universe, and our well-being with the well-being of the planet.

Franciscan spirituality is a treasure trove of practices, grounded in the call to proclaim peace to all creation. In greeting our human and non-human companions with peace, we take the first steps toward transforming our relationships and political activities. "Peace is the way," even in the scrum of diversity, conflict, and compromise. To see the best in ourselves and others paves the way for a world in which we study war no more. Peace is connected to praise. Praise is recognition of the dynamic and graceful interdependence of life resounding in all creation, calling us to a sensate spirituality in which we find God in all creation and all creation in God. While not obvious at first glance, holy poverty and simplicity reflect and nurture the quest for peace in our lives and the world. Holy poverty enables us to prune away everything that stands between us and God and us and our human and non-human kin. Holy poverty encourages simplicity in our inner and outer lives, and thus lessons unhealthy anxiety and busyness. The Danish philosopher Søren Kierkegaard counsels "purity of heart is to will one thing," that is, to let the quest to experience and honor God's presence in our lives and companions be our primary intention. Today, we live out the quest for holiness in seeking justice for all creation and putting care for the Earth and its creatures as our motivation in every aspect of our lives from business to family decision-making.

Clare invites us to "gaze" at the life of Jesus, his ministry, healing, and crucifixion and resurrection and let Jesus' life be the polestar of our decision-making and lifestyle. When Clare invites the regal Agnes of Prague to "imitate" Jesus, she encourages her to see Jesus as her model and embody Jesus' empathetic spirit and willingness to suffer for the healing of the world. Today, taking up our cross means living more simply, putting the well-being of the planet above profit and power, and sharing power with the vulnerable and marginalized. It means privileging others' well-being as much as our own and dying to self-interest to be reborn in the fullness of God's love. It inspires us to the largeness of self, described by Whitehead, in which our interests are joined lovingly with the interests of those around us and our selves enlarge to embrace the whole Earth.

Bonaventure teaches us to immerse ourselves in the flow of God's love, opening to God's fountain of light and love through a process of loving the world and then letting our love for the world lead us to unity of spirit with the One in whom all things live and move and have their being. Cultivating awareness of beauty awakens us to Divine Beauty and inspires us to be beauty seekers and beauty makers. Bonaventure's spirituality of ascent involves self-transcendence and focus on God and then returning to our daily life open to God's presence in every encounter and every creature. The journey of the soul, like the angels of Jacob's Ladder, begins on Earth, ascends to the heavens, and returns to Earth filled with intent on doing God's will "on Earth as it is in heaven."

Now more than ever, we are challenged to see that we are the ones that we have been waiting for. While we may seem unimportant as we gaze at photos from the Hubble and Webb telescopes, every place, including our lives is centered in God, and everything we do can reflect and further God's vision of the universe. Rabbi

Abraham Joshua Heschel reminds us that Jewish mystics believed that when you save a soul, it's as if you save the world; when you destroy a soul, it's as if you've destroyed the world. I believe that the world is saved one action at a time. Our moment-by-moment actions and commitments can further the spiritual and moral arcs of history and support God's dream of healing the earth. We can choose to become God's companions in healing the Earth and bringing peace on Earth and goodwill to all.

SPIRITUAL PRACTICES FOR GLOBAL HEALERS

We are the ones we've been waiting for. "This is the day that God has made" and on this day, we can commit to being peacemakers and healers. We can rejoice and create conditions that make joy possible for others. We can be saints-in-the-making, immersed in the earth and caring for future generations. These mantras energize this text and our lives.

Good Ancestors in the Making. Yoruba religion describes good ancestors as persons of goodness and integrity who shape our lives from beyond the grave. The love in this life continues in the afterlife, flooding back into the world in healing ways. If we follow the paths of the three saints –Francis, Bonaventure, and Clare – and "Saint Alfred," we will live each day to its fullest in light of the everlasting impact of our actions. We will practice being good ancestors in the making, for "just such a time as this." In practice, this means:

- Living intentionally and mindfully moment by moment.
- Cultivating a peaceful and prayerful demeanor.
- Treating each person you meet as divine.
- Praying for political leaders including those with whom you disagree.
- Protesting injustice gracefully and lovingly.
- Living your life in the now with consideration for future generations.

The world is healed by one act and encounter at a time and one act can change the lives of another person or our own lives and push forward the movements of the moral and spiritual arcs of history.

Something Beautiful for God. Beauty is at the heart of Franciscan and Whiteheadian spirituality. Whitehead asserts that the aim of the universe – God's aim – at the production of beauty. Following Francis' Canticle, Bonaventure sees all things as vestiges of divine love and wisdom and states that earthly beauty reflects and leads us toward the experience of divine beauty. Within the world of the flesh, we are challenged to be beauty and see beauty, or as Mother (Saint) Teresa says, "do something beautiful for God." In the course of the days ahead:

- Notice beauty everywhere.
- Notice the impact of your actions on those around you.
- Commit to being a beauty-maker in every encounter.
- Delight in the wonder and beauty of your life and the lives of those around you.
- Say "thank you" to God and everyone who adds to the goodness of your life and the world.
- As a citizen, make a commitment to nurturing the politics and economics of beauty in your political advocacy and involvement.

Let us go forth today and tomorrow knowing that this is our moment, we are the ones we've been waiting for, as God's instruments of peace. Go in peace, treasuring God and all things, and healing the world one act at a time.

BOOKS TO NOURISH THE SPIRIT

Texts on Franciscan Spirituality

Bonaventure, *The Soul's Journey into God, The Tree of Life, The Life of St. Francis,* translation and introduction by Ewert Cousins, Paulist Press, 1978.

Murray Bodo, *Francis: The Journey and the Dream: Fortieth Anniversary Edition,* Franciscan Media, 2012.

Murray Bodo, *Surrounded by Love: Seven Teachings of St. Francis,* Franciscan Media, 2018.

Ilia Delio, *Clare of Assisi: Heart Full of Love,* Franciscan Media, 2007.

Ilia Delio, *Compassion: Living in the Spirit of St. Francis,* Franciscan Media, 2011.

Ilia Delio, *Crucified Love: Bonaventure's Mysticism of the Crucified Christ*, Franciscan Media, 1999.

Ilia Delio, *Franciscan Prayer,* Franciscan Media, 2004.

Ilia Delio, *Simply Bonaventure: An Introduction to His Life, Thought, and Writings,* New City Press, 2001.

Ilia Delio, *The Humility of God: A Franciscan Perspective,* Franciscan Media, 2006.

Bruce Epperly, *Head, Heart, and Hands: An Introduction to St. Bonaventure.* Cincinnati, OH: Franciscan Media, 2024.

Bruce Epperly, *Simplicity, Spirituality, Service: The Timeless Wisdom of Francis, Clare, and Bonaventure,* Franciscan Media, 2023.

Bruce Epperly, *Walking with Francis of Assisi: From Privilege to Activism,* Franciscan Media, 2021.

Francis of Assisi, *Francis of Assisi: The Saint – The Early Documents.* Edited by Regis Armstrong. Hyde Park, NY: New City Press, 1999.

Richard Rohr, *Eager to Love: The Alternative Way of Francis of Assisi,* Franciscan Media, 2016.

Andre Vauchez, *Francis of Assisi: The Life and Afterlife of a Medieval Saint* (New Haven: Yale University Press, 2016).

Texts on Whiteheadian Spirituality

Daniel Dombrowski, *Process Mysticism.* Albany, NY: SUNY Press, 2023.

Bruce Epperly, *Homegrown Mystics: American Spiritual Visionaries.* Vestal, NY: Anamchara Books, 2024.

_____, *The God of the Growing Edges: Whitehead and Teilhard on Theology, Spirituality, and Social Change.* Gonzalez, FL: Energion Publications, 2024.

_____, *The God of Tomorrow: Whitehead on Metaphysics, Mysticism, and Mission.* Gonzalez, FL: Energion Publications, 2024.

_____, *Jesus: Mystic, Healer, and Prophet.* Anamchara Books, 2023.

_____, *Mystics in Action: Twelve Saints for Today.* Maryknoll, NY: Orbis Books, 2020.

_____, *Process Theology: A Guide for the Perplexed.* London: Continuum, 2011.

_____, *Process Theology and Mysticism*. Gonzalez, FL: _Energion, 2024.

_____, *Process Theology and Politics*. Gonzalez, FL: Energion, 2020.

_____, *Process Theology and Prophetic Faith*. Gonzalez, FL: Energion, 2024.

_____, *Process Theology: Embracing Adventure with God*. Gonzalez, FL: Energion, 2014.

_____, *The Mystic in You: Discovering a God-filled World*. Nashville: Upper Room Books, 2018.

_____, *We are All Mystics: How Spirituality Can Save Your Life and the World*, Anamchara Books, 2024.

_____, *The God of Tomorrow: Whitehead and Teilhard on Metaphysics, Mystics, and Mission*. Gonzalez, F, 2024.L

Victor Lowe, *Alfred North Whitehead: The Man and His Work*. Baltimore: Johns Hopkins Press, 1985.

Whitehead, Alfred North. *Adventures of Ideas*. Paperback. New York: The Free Press, 1933.

_____, *The Function of Reason*. Boston: Beacon Press, 1969.

_____, Mathematics and the Good" and "Immorality," *The Philosophy of Alfred North Whitehead: Library of Living Philosophers,* volume 3, Paul Arthur Schilpp, editor. Evanston, IL: Northwestern University Press, 1941

_____, *Modes of Thought*. New York: The Free Press, 1968.

_____. *Process and Reality: Corrected Edition*. Edited by David Ray Griffin and Donald W. Sherburne. New York: The Free Press, 1979.

_____, *Religion in the Making*. New York: Meridian, 1960.

_____, *Science and the Modern World*. New York: Free Press, 1967